Power and Powerlessness: The Injustice of India's Electricity System

Power and Powerlessness: The Injustice of India's Electricity System

Social Research Collective

First Published 2018

ISBN 978-93-83723-24-9

Published by
LG PUBLISHERS DISTRIBUTORS
49, Street No. 14, Pratap Nagar,
Mayur Vihar Phase I, Delhi 110 091
Email: lgpdist@gmail.com

Designed by
Limited Colors, Delhi 110 092

Printed at
D.K. Fine Art Press, Delhi 110 052

Contents

1
Introduction

If you were to ask most people in India today about what they mean by "development", you would probably get two basic answers: roads and electricity. The reason is obvious. Electricity is a basic need for practically all people, and it is also one of the most obvious failures of infrastructure in India today. Power cuts, load shedding, voltage fluctuations, and simple lack of electricity supply are basic features of life for the vast majority of Indians. At the same time, and with far less attention from the media, electricity-related projects—dams, coal mines, power plants—have sparked conflicts across India. In both ways, electricity is a central issue in policy and politics across the entire country.

In this book, we try to look at the electricity sector from this broader perspective. We seek to ask—why is India's electricity sector failing in so many different ways? What are the common threads between these myriad failures? Perhaps most importantly, what can those who care about justice, dignity and development do about those failures?

The answers we have found are not what one might expect. The structure of the modern electricity sector in India hides more than it reveals, and there is a giant gap between the stated goals of that structure and the actual reality of the policies, institutions, rules and guidelines that make it work. In Chapter 2 of this book, we will first discuss this formal structure. Chapters 3, 4 and 5 look at the key parts of the electricity system—generation, transmission and distribution—and the spiralling conflicts and contradictions developing around each of them. Chapter 5 also discusses the findings of a field survey we conducted across four regions of three states, which sought to test some common conceptions of the electricity sector against the experiences of poor and working class people. Chapter 6 then examines the functioning of the regulatory commissions, which set tariffs for generation, transmission and distribution of electricity. Chapter 7 ties these threads together into an overall picture of the problems in the electricity system; and, finally, Chapter 8 explores what these findings mean for understanding future steps for India's electricity sector—and what can be done, at multiple levels, for addressing the injustice and exploitation with which it is so closely bound.

This book is neither a policy manual nor a technical report on the electricity sector—we aim instead to present a kind of map of this system. We hope that the findings here can be useful at multiple levels—to individuals, such as researchers, academics and those simply interested in the subject; to organisations working for social justice in local areas or at regional and state levels; and to groups fighting for larger-scale policy changes. Where we were aware of technical information or additional resources that may be useful to the reader, we have referred to them either in a footnote or in our bibliography.

1. Where India's Electricity Sector is in 2017

As we write this, state elections have just concluded in five states, including Uttar Pradesh, India's largest state. While general election surveys tend to ask voters to prioritise between "development" or "security" or similar broad concepts, one data journalism group did a much more specific survey in

Uttar Pradesh. Unsurprisingly, the top concern that emerged among voters was "power cuts".[1]

Dissatisfaction with electricity supply is an issue that cuts across castes, communities, regions, states, and classes in India—with the sole exception of the urban rich who can afford generator backup, almost everyone else has to face unreliable and often unavailable supply. An estimated 400 million people in India still have no access to electricity at all.[2] While government data claims rapidly climbing electrification figures, these are based on extremely loose criteria. For instance, if 10% of the households as well as public buildings in a village have electricity connections, the village is deemed 'electrified'—regardless of whether even those connections receive any supply.[3] This results in statistics like Madhya Pradesh and Jharkhand claiming electrification rates of 97% and 93% respectively, while satellite data shows that large areas of these states are almost completely dark at night.[4] Among others, as our field survey showed, the vast majority of people experience a significant power cut daily, and in many areas one to two hour cuts at the least are a daily reality. Voltage fluctuations further affect equipment, appliances and the usefulness of electricity supply as well.

Meanwhile, electricity supply has become a central issue for almost all political parties in India. During his 2014 election campaign, the current Prime Minister, Narendra Modi, often cited achievements in ensuring full electrification in Gujarat as a major achievement (though this was not in fact true). When the "nuclear deal" between the then United Progressive Alliance government and the US government was becoming controversial in 2008, Rahul Gandhi, then Vice President of the Congress, made an example of how the deal would ensure electricity supply even to the most marginalised—his example being an adivasi woman named Kalavati. Similarly, in Tamil Nadu, in the wake of protests against the nuclear power plant in Kudankulam, Chief Minister Jayalalitha argued that the plant would ensure electricity to all in the state and that those protesting were hence "anti-development."

This political centrality is a key issue in making the electricity system work the way it does—a point we will return to in Chapter 7. But electricity is central to the Indian polity in two other ways as well.

The first is the takeover of land, mineral and water resources for 'development projects', a major issue that is now spiralling into conflicts across India. A large proportion of these projects are electricity-related. For instance, in an earlier prediction, Yudhvir Singh[5] applied the Planning Commission's estimates of the amount of land required for a coal mine to the government's mining targets, and estimated that the projected mining expansion would require an additional 593,790 hectares of land (the vast majority of coal mining is for thermal power plants). Between 2006 and 2011 alone, environment clearances for an additional 583 million tonnes of mining were granted[6]—more than the existing mining capacity in 2006. Hydroelectric power is at a similarly dizzying scale. The 2008 Hydro Power Policy sets a target of generating 66,000 megawatts from the Brahmaputra basin alone and states that the country's potential hydropower generation capacity is more than five times the capacity of current projects. Hence, more than 150 dams were earlier planned in Arunachal Pradesh[7] and over 500 hydropower related projects are planned in Uttarakhand.[8] Each of these projects involves taking over land, often involves the destruction of forests and local ecosystems, disrupts and almost always destroys the livelihoods of local communities, and has wider implications for the environment. Even renewable energy, in particular the planned massive expansion in "solar farms", will require considerable land.

Naturally, this means that electricity-related projects end up being at the centre of the spiralling clash between state agencies and those opposing takeover of their resources. This is the case even though it is clear that many of these projects are never going to come into existence, since the takeover of land or the grant of mining leases is often done in any case (even if the project is not completed). This point is discussed further in Chapter 3 below.

Finally, the electricity sector is also at the centre of another hidden conflict in India today—the "bad loans" problem, or the large number of loans taken from banks that are not being repaid on time. This is threatening the stability of the entire Indian financial system, and power sector projects are at the centre of it. In 2015, for instance, the Reserve Bank of India's Financial Stability Report noted that power sector projects accounted for 29.31% of "restructured standard advances"—or loans whose payment schedule had to be extended—despite the fact that the sector only accounted for 9.24% of total loans.[9] Both generating and distribution companies have taken such loans.[10]

In short, the electricity sector is currently at the centre of multiple crises. What should be done about this?

2. The "Standard Model" of Analysis

Given all these problems, the electricity sector has been the subject of an extensive debate in the media and in policy circles. However, voices close to the government, international financial institutions, policy think tanks and most media commentators have largely converged on one set of key problems in the electricity system—and hence one set of prescriptions for remedying them.[11]

The first of these prescriptions is—or rather was, till recently—increasing generation capacity, on the argument that this will address the unreliability, limited nature and low quality of electricity supply. Indeed, almost all policy documents between 2003 and 2015 reflect this approach. For instance, the National Electricity Policy of 2005 identifies "substantial peak and energy shortages", with an urgent need to increase generation, as a key problem in the sector.[12] Similarly, as discussed above, the National Hydroelectricity Policy of 2008 targets a fivefold expansion in India's hydroelectric power generation. In 2005, McKinsey predicted that meeting demand would require a "five to tenfold increase in the pace of capacity addition [in generation]".[13]

The second is to complete the 'incomplete' process of privatising distribution and transmission companies. As discussed in Chapter 2, under the 2003 Electricity Act, these functions were supposed to be "unbundled" and handed over to private companies. But till date only two states have privatised their distribution companies—Odisha and Delhi—along with a handful of cities; and transmission remains an almost total government monopoly. Moreover, Delhi and Odisha had privatised their discoms prior to the Electricity Act. While private projects in the transmission sector are accelerating,[14] no state has announced any move towards privatising its discoms.

This "failure to privatise" is then blamed for the power sector's other major problems. Since the power distribution companies are owned by the state, it is argued, they are subject to political pressure and are not permitted to take steps that might make the government unpopular. Examples include the continuation of free electricity for agricultural purposes in most states, "artificially low" tariffs that do not permit cost recovery, and an ostensible failure to crackdown on power thieves and to ensure all connections are metreed. This in turn pushes the discoms deep into debt, imperilling their financial health and that of the banks and other financial institutions that have given them credit. They also do not invest in better equipment, resulting in higher losses and supply failures. In this view, privatisation would result in a virtuous cycle of higher tariffs, better discom finances, higher investment, and so on. Even if privatisation is not possible, in this view, higher tariffs are a must.

In sum, over the past decade, supporters of this 'standard model' have broadly pushed three basic prescriptions: increase generation capacity through easier regulations and incentives for private investment; hike tariffs; and/or privatise distribution companies while accelerating private investment in transmission.

Much government policy is driven by these assumptions. For instance, as discussed in the section on generation, there is a steady process of dilution and easing of regulatory restrictions that are argued to be "interfering" with private investment in generation. The central government's UDAY scheme (discussed in the Chapter on distribution below), intended to rescue state government-owned discoms from debt, includes a number of conditions, foremost of which is that prices should be adjusted quarterly to address fuel price changes and that annual increases should be required.[15] It is important to note that these policies have remained in place even as, over time, the prescriptions of the standard model have become either outdated or seem increasingly incomplete.

3. Problems in the Picture

At first glance, the standard model seems to make perfect sense. But look more closely and several problems begin to arise—enough to give us reason to question the logic underlying this entire picture.

The first problem is that lack of generation capacity has suddenly ceased to be a problem. Compared to the targets that were suggested for the needed increase in generation capacity, the actual electricity demand from discoms seems to have not risen anywhere near as quickly as was predicted. As of December 2016, official data indicates that India's overall energy deficit is only 0.7% (with a deficit at peak demand times of 1.6%)—as compared to 10.1% as recently as 2010.[16] Moreover, the data also shows a steady decline in the "plant load factor"—namely the amount of electricity a plant has actually produced in a given period, as a fraction of its theoretical capacity. Whereas this averaged 77.5% for all plants in 2009-2010, it had fallen sharply to 59.6% in the April-December 2016 period.[17] Private sector plants had shown a particularly sharp fall over the same period, with their PLF dropping from 83.9% in 2009-2010 to 56.3% in 2016—a fall of 27 percentage points. In 2016, both state government and private sector plants had PLFs that were only slightly over half (53% and 56% respectively). In other words, power deficits have reached such a low level that many generation plants are literally running only half the time.

We should clarify here that this data refers to demand for electricity from *distribution companies* (discoms), not necessarily from the public as a whole. As we noted above, there are still huge numbers of households who are not even connected to the grid, and who would presumably expand this demand if they were able to access electricity. But, as discussed below, that only adds to the paradox.

The government has acknowledged the current reality by sharply revising its own proposed capacity targets downwards. As we were writing this in December 2016, the government published a new draft National Electricity Plan which, among other changes, sets a projected peak demand of 317 gigawatts in 2026-2027. This is roughly 20% lower than previous targets.[18] Applying a variety of prediction models, the draft plan also says that in all foreseeable scenarios no new coal power plants—still India's main power source—need be built other than those already under construction, after almost two decades of policies that offered incentives, cheap land, easy clearances and regulatory dilution for coal powered plants in the name of addressing India's energy shortage.

Meanwhile, the underutilisation of generation capacity is only one half of the paradox of electricity generation in India. The other is the fact that a great deal of new generation projects have been planned on paper, and often both cleared and financed—that are unlikely to ever come into existence. For instance, in 2012, the Chhattisgarh private power producers' association estimated that only sixteen out of a planned 45 private power generating plants in the state are likely to ever come up.[19] As of 2013, the Arunachal Pradesh government had signed so many public private partnership deals for hydropower projects in the state that it would have had to spend over four times its annual budget to meet its commitments to these projects.[20] Similar stories abound, as we discuss in Chapter 3 below. Further, even in the most recent plan, the targets for mining coal have remained the same—meaning that we are soon going to be producing far more coal than can be consumed.[21]

In other words, the generation part of the electricity system seems to be in a peculiar fix—with very large plans on paper, smaller plans in practice, and insufficient demand to justify either. Why has this happened? Especially at a time when large numbers of households still do not have electricity connections (48.22 lakh households in Madhya Pradesh alone, as of early 2016[22]).

The reasons appear to be twofold. First, the lack of enough of an increase in transmission capacity to take the power from these generation plants.[23] Second, more importantly, the lack of demand from distribution companies. This in turn leads us back to the question of why the discoms are in such a financial mess, and why, in turn, electricity demand remains so low.

The standard prescription here—privatisation—does not actually answer either of these problems. Prices are already fixed by regulators, not by either governments or discoms. If the assumption is that the regulator is being politically pressured, then that pressure will apply whether or not the distribution company is private. If the assumption is that the discom is not even asking for a tariff that is appropriate because it is under pressure, that goes against the record, where regulators frequently *reduce* the discom's asking rate—meaning that discoms are bidding too high, not too low (see the discussion in Chapter 6). Even if this was not the case, if the assumption is that a private distributor would be able to massively hike tariffs, such a move may trigger a popular backlash, with ensuing political consequences.[24]

Further, this entire discourse is premised on the idea that there is such a thing as a transparent "cost" that can easily be estimated and "recovered". As we shall see in Chapters 6 and 7, there is widespread financial mismanagement in both private and public discoms that results in their 'costs'—both estimated and actual—being inflated beyond the necessary. The same is true of private generating companies' tariffs, some of whom, as discussed in Chapter 7, are currently under investigation for outright fraud. Much of the standard model discourse also commits a basic category mistake—it conflates *means,* such as efficient, cost-effective, commercial discoms, with the *end,* which is reliable, high quality electricity supply to those who need it. Full cost recovery for a discom is of no use if the discom does not supply electricity properly, or if most of the population receives no supply.

Thus, at the end of the day, the standard prescriptions fail entirely to answer two basic questions. First, if this regulatory system—independent regulators fixing tariffs on the basis of a guaranteed "return on investment" (or ostensibly on competitive bidding)—is the solution, why is it not working right now? Why is it failing to address any of the serious problems in India's electricity sector? Is it enough, for the purposes of analysis, to simply lament some vague "lack of political will"?

Or are the problems deeper?

4. The Approach of This Book

In this book, we attempt to take a step back and start from a different position from the standard approach discussed above. We start with a more basic question: how is electricity produced, supplied and distributed in India? Who controls each step in the chain? What are the power dynamics around each step, and how do they impact the system as a whole?

This is, in other words, a *political economy analysis* of the electricity sector in India.[25] We argue that at each step, questions about political power and accountability are vital to understanding why the system works—or does not work—in the manner that it does.

In the next Chapter we start this exploration by looking at the basic institutional structure of the electricity system in India. Subsequent Chapters look at the various parts of this system in more detail.

Endnotes

1. Shreya Shah, "One Third of UP Voters Polled Cite Power Cuts as Leading Election Issue," *India Spend* (6 February 2017).
2. ET, "India's Looming Power Crisis," *Economic Times* (19 February 2016).
3. Anuj Srivas, "It's Time to Shift the Rural Electrification Goalpost," *The Wire* (12 April 2016).
4. Jahnavi Sen, "The Social Realities of India's Electrification, in One Map," *The Wire* (24 January 2016).
5. "Presentation to National Consultation on Takeover of Common Lands" (Society for Promotion of Wasteland Development, July 2011).
6. CSE, "Coal Mining" (Centre for Science and Environment, 22 September 2011), http://www.cseindia.org/userfiles/Coal%20mining.pdf.
7. Jason Overdorf, "How Many Dams Can One State Hold?" *Global Post* (2012), http://www.globalpost.com/dispatch/news/regions/asia-pacific/india/120315/dam-nation-arunachal-pradesh-hydropower-electricity-part-1.
8. Rakesh Agarwal, "Hydropower Projects in Uttarakhand," *Economic and Political Weekly* 48, No. 29 (20 July 2013).
9. RBI, *Financial Stability Report* (Reserve Bank of India, Reserve Bank of India, 2015).

10. Sheoli Pargal and Sudeshna Ghosh Banerjee, *More Power to India: The Challenge of Electricity Distribution* (World Bank, 2014).
11. Some examples of reports / commentary that take this approach can be found in ibid., KPMG, *Power Sector in India: White Paper on Challenges in Implementation and Opportunities* (KPMG, 2010), ET, "How Uday Is Going to Help Transform India's Power Distribution System," *Economic Times* (25 October 2016) and ET, "India's Looming Power Crisis.".
12. Paragraph 1.4.
13. McKinsey, *Powering India: The Road to 2017* (McKinsey Co., 2005).
14. Pargal and Banerjee, *More Power to India.*
15. Shishir Asthana, "UDAY Is a Revival Plan for Discoms Rather Than a Bailout Package," *Business Standard* (6 November 2015).
16. Data confirmed from the website of the Ministry of Power on 15 February, 2017.
17. Ibid.
18. Armin Rosencranz and Rajnish Wadehra, "The Confusion Over Coal, Power Tells Us India Hasn't Outgrown the Need for Planning," *The Wire* (18 February 2017).
19. M. Rajshekhar, "Chhattisgarh Power Boom That Never Was: Only 15 Out 60 Thermal Plants May Get Operational," *Economic Times* (25 October 2012).
20. M. Rajshekhar, "Hydelgate: Why Arunachal Pradesh's Hydel Boom Is Going Bust," *Economic Times* (30 April 2013).
21. Rosencranz and Wadehra, "The Confusion over Coal, Power Tells Us India Hasn't Outgrown the Need for Planning."
22. Srivas, "It's Time to Shift the Rural Electrification Goalpost."
23. Nityanand Jayaraman and Mukul Kumar, "There is No Power Shortage in the Country—But the Entire Sector is in a Mess," *Scroll.in* (18 August 2016), https://scroll.in/article/814192/there-is-no-power-shortage-in-the-country-but-the-entire-sector-is-in-a-mess.
24. For instance, power tariff hikes were rolled back in Rajasthan in February 2017, in Bihar in March 2017, and in Tamil Nadu in April 2012 after protests.
25. We draw inspiration for this approach from the "system of provision" approach adopted by Ben Fine and Ellen Leopold in their 1993 book *The World of Consumption,* Ben Fine and Ellen Leopold, *The World of Consumption* (Routledge, 1993). They argue that the supply chain for a commodity—in our case, electricity—is not just a technical set of steps that provides "consumers" with something they "demand." In reality, what people 'demand' is not independent of what is available, and what is available is not dependent only on what is demanded (or on what is technically possible). For instance, whether people use electricity and how much they use is not independent of the quality of electricity supply, the number and length of power cuts, the corruption involved in getting a connection, and so on. Similarly, how much is generated is not, as discussed above, just a function of whether coal and permissions are available. Rather, the system functions as a whole, with each step influencing the previous and succeeding ones. It is the whole system that has certain inherent tendencies, not each step on its own.

2

The Structure of India's Electricity Sector

Just after India won independence in 1947, the first national legislation on electricity was passed—the Electricity Act of 1948. It established the State Electricity Boards, each of which were responsible for the generation, transmission and distribution of electricity within their state, and also created the Central Electricity Authority as an advisory body for planning and policymaking. In 1950 the new Constitution included electricity as a "concurrent subject" where both the central and the state governments had jurisdiction; and in 1956 the central government formally nationalised the electricity sector, leaving only the existing private sector leases and licensees to continue their operations.[1]

This wholly government controlled electricity system continued to operate until 1991. At the time, India had a peak energy deficit of around 18%, transmission and distribution losses of approximately 23% and a plant load factor of 54%; and an electrification rate of approximately 42%.[2] These figures are important, as they are what we would measure against when considering the level of "improvement" following the sweeping changes to the electricity sector that have taken place in the following 25 years.

After the foreign exchange crisis in 1991 led to the onset of what we now refer to as "liberalisation", steps were initiated to increase private participation in the power sector. The first of these was to permit "Independent Power Producers" (IPPs), or private power generating plants. But these did not go very far—by 2002, they still only generated 3% of India's electricity.[3] In 1996, Odisha passed the Odisha Electricity Reform Act, becoming the first state in the country to "unbundle" its electricity board into separate generation, transmission and distribution sections and setting up a regulatory commission to set tariffs. Following the same model, in 1998 the central government passed the Electricity Regulatory Commissions Act to set up state level regulatory commissions and the Central Electricity Regulatory Commission. Most states set up their regulatory commissions the following year, and Odisha also privatised electricity distribution in the state (leading, incidentally, to a scandal when the private electricity distributor in the state failed to restore power for months following the 1999 supercyclone[4]). In 2002, Delhi followed Odisha's lead and became the second state to privatise distribution, handing over distribution licenses to two private companies.

1. The 2003 Electricity Act

All this led up to the passage, in 2003, of the omnibus Electricity Act by the then National Democratic Alliance government. The new Act was meant to replace all the preceding "piecemeal reforms" with a single, comprehensive legislation that would lay down the basic structure and key objectives of India's electricity system.

The Act formalised and publicly declared the essential focus of the new electricity system. The 'preamble' of the legislation—the first paragraph of the Act, which states its purpose—reads as follows:

> An Act to consolidate the laws relating to generation, transmission, distribution, trading and use of electricity and generally for taking measures conducive to development of electricity industry, promoting competition therein, protecting interest of consumers and supply of electricity to all areas, rationalisation of electricity tariff, ensuring transparent policies regarding subsidies, promotion of efficient and environmentally benign policies, constitution of Central Electricity Authority, Regulatory Commissions and establishment of Appellate Tribunal and for matters connected to ...

Certain words leap out here—"competition"; "transparency"; "rationalisation"; "protecting interest of consumers"; "development of the electricity industry". In essence, the new regime was to be driven by the major goal of increasing the accountability and efficiency of the sector. The method chosen for this purpose was to facilitate and encourage the involvement of private sector companies.

These goals are important, as most later analyses—especially those that fit into the 'standard model' described in the previous chapter—take these goals and this approach for granted. As we shall see, in practice neither these goals nor this method of approaching them has proven unproblematic.

In order to set up this new structure, the Act first required the "unbundling" of the State Electricity Boards into separate transmission and distribution companies (as well as generation companies if the state board was involved in generation). Even if these new companies remained under government ownership, they were technically independent companies. In Uttarakhand, for instance, the distribution component of the Board was hived off as the Uttarakhand Power Corporation Ltd. (UPCL), and the transmission part was converted into the Power Transmission Corporation of Uttaranchal (PTCUL).

The new Act then set out certain basic principles for each part of the unbundled electricity supply chain.

For *generation*, the Act held that generation would now be "delicensed" and opened to private investment. Henceforth, a private company or any other entity wishing to generate power would not require any government permissions for the act of generating electricity as such (they might require permissions under other laws, such as environment and forest clearances, for instance). The only exception to this principle are large hydroelectric projects, which continue to require permission from the Central Electricity Authority.

Once set up, how does the generation company sell its electricity? For it to do so, the generation plant has three options, discussed in further detail in Chapter 3 below. The first is to sell its power to a company or entity with a distribution license, usually through a long-term power purchase agreement (PPA), at tariffs fixed by the respective Regulatory Commissions (see below). The second is to sell its power on what is called the "spot market", where power trading companies buy and sell power "on the spot" (i.e. as and when needed). The rates for such power are unregulated. The third is to use its power locally as a captive power plant for a particular industry; it was later clarified (in 2005) that at least 51% of the electricity should be used in-house for the plant to qualify as a captive plant.[5] The remainder of the electricity generated by such plants can be sold, again, through either PPAs or on the spot market.

Physically, however, transmitting the electricity from the place it is generated to the place it is distributed requires a transmission network. For this, the Act provided for "opening" of the transmission sector as well. Any private or government company can engage in transmission activities, but unlike in the case of generation, this would require the company to first obtain a license from the regulatory commission. The Act requires that any licensee for transmission of electricity would have to do so with an 'open access' model—meaning that it cannot discriminate between either generation plants or between distribution licensees, and would have to carry everyone's electricity for equal rates. Transmission licensees also cannot generate or trade electricity. Transmission licensees can charge fees—known as "wheeling charges"—for transmission of electricity, but the rates for such charges are fixed by the Regulatory Commissions (see below). The overall transmission system is operated through what are known as state, regional and national dispatch centres (described in more detail in Chapter 4). The Act mandates that dispatch centres should either be government entities or run by companies specifically contracted to do so by the government.

In addition to the transmission network, the Act also creates a new category of licensees known as power traders—companies empowered to act as exchanges between distribution companies and generation companies, and to arrange for the spot purchase of electricity from the latter by the former. The charges that these companies can levy are also fixed by the regulatory commissions.

Once the electricity reaches close to its point of destination, the transmission licensee hands it over to the third and final leg of the supply chain—the distribution company. Distribution, like transmission, requires a license.[6] Distribution companies are expected to distribute the electricity to final consumers, including households, industries, government agencies, and so on. For this purpose the distribution company can charge a tariff, but that tariff has to be approved by the Regulatory Commission. The Act mandates that consumers taking more than one megawatt of electricity—essentially industries and large structures—must be allowed to choose which company they receive it from (also known as an "open access" model). But other consumers need not be given a choice; while the Act envisaged a competitive environment between distribution licensees, that was not made mandatory, and it has not materialised. Finally, in 2014, proposals were made to amend the Act to include a fourth stage in the supply process—namely "supply" licensees, discussed further in Chapter 5—but this has not yet been passed.

To supervise and regulate these three steps in the chain—generation, transmission and distribution—the Act also mandated that every state should have a State Electricity Regulatory Commission, along with a Central Electricity Regulatory Commission. These commissions have a number of responsibilities. The first is to set the rates for "generation, supply, transmission and wheeling of electricity" (Section 86). Companies that supply electricity across states can have their rates set by the Central Commission, but in practice all rates appear to be set by the state commissions. In addition, the commissions are responsible for issuing licenses for transmission, distribution and power trading, for encouraging use of renewable sources of electricity by fixing minimum quotas, and for regulating the system in general within their state or (in the case of the Central Commission) the country as a whole. The act then also provides for the constitution of an Appellate Tribunal to hear appeals against the decisions of the Regulatory Commissions.

Of these tasks, fixing rates and prices for electricity is the most fundamental. The actual procedure followed to set these rates is discussed in Chapter 6, and is scattered across multiple legal instruments, from the Electricity Act to various policies (see below) and court judgments. But Section 61 of the Electricity Act lays down the basic principles that need to be kept in mind. The Commissions are mandated to be "guided" by the following: that "generation, transmission and supply of electricity should be conducted on commercial principles"; "safeguarding of consumers' interest and at the same time, recovery of the cost of electricity in a reasonable manner"; "rewarding efficiency in performance"; "encourag[ing] competition, efficiency, economical use of resources, good performance and optimum investments"; "reflecting the cost of supply of electricity"; and so on.

As can be seen, the repeated invocation of "commercial" and "cost" in these sections sends a clear message—the tariffs have to cover costs. But this then has to be "balanced" against "consumers' interest." This idea of "balancing" is at the heart of the entire structure of the Act. The regulatory commissions, in this understanding, function like a kind of specialised court whose job is to hear 'both' sides regarding tariffs and fix them in such a way as to balance these interests. This will ensure that the producers have enough money to invest, maintain and operate their systems, on the one hand, and that they are not permitted to fleece people on the other. It is also assumed that this will ensure that the system is transparent, accountable and efficient, since all sides will be heard.

In practice, as we saw, this does not seem to be happening. The reasons for this are discussed in the rest of this book.

2. The Operational Machinery: Policies, Laws and Rulings

On its own the Electricity Act merely sets out the broad framework of the electricity system. The actual operation of the system relies on a much more complicated set of legal instruments. These include the following:

- National policies not mandated by law: These include the National Electricity Policy of 2005 (currently under revision), the National Hydropower Policy of 2008 and so on. These documents set out the broad goals of government policy and state targets, such as the goal of increasing India's hydropower potential by five times, and so on.
- National policies mandated by law: The Electricity Act specifically requires the Central Electricity Authority

and the Central Electricity Regulatory Commission to issue certain policy documents on a regular basis. These include the National Tariff Policy (which governs tariff setting by regulators) and the National Electricity Plan, which has to be revised every five years. Unlike the preceding category of policies, these documents have more legal force, as they are required by law.

- Orders and rules of regulatory commissions: Under the Electricity Act, the regulatory commissions are also empowered to make their own regulations. Most follow the rules and orders issued by the Central Electricity Regulatory Commission in this regard. These are issued at various times and usually available on the commissions' websites. These orders include regulations and policies for fixing tariffs; the quota of renewable energy that every distribution company has to purchase (the so-called renewable purchase obligation, discussed further in the next chapter); and other rulings within the commissions' jurisdiction.
- Orders of the dispatch centres: The dispatch centres are also empowered to issue orders to transmission licensees and other entities on the network, and these are binding.
- Rulings of ombudsmen and tribunals: The Appellate Tribunal (Electricity) can pass orders in appeals against decisions of the regulatory commissions. In addition, states have ombudsmen, or independent officials whose job is to respond to consumer complaints. These orders are also binding on distribution companies, though they are usually passed in individual cases rather than on policies.
- Rulings of courts: Finally, many of these issues are taken to court—above all on the questions of tariffs and pricing. Sometimes these court cases come from appeals against

decisions of the appellate tribunals, and sometimes they are directly raised before High Courts or the Supreme Court through writ petitions. These judgments in turn are binding.

To detail all these policies, rulings, orders and documents would require an encyclopedia of its own. In this book, we will be focusing on key provisions that have had an impact, and will refer to them where relevant in the Chapters below.

But it is important to note that one of the key features of India's electricity system today is precisely the sheer amount of legal and regulatory complexity that it brings with it. There are several authorities with different but often overlapping jurisdictions, passing orders, regulations and policies that are not always publicly available, and of which many actors in the system—apart from those outside it—are not always aware themselves. This is, of course, one reason for books like this, which seek to act as a map to the key issues in this morass of documentation. But it is also a political feature of the system itself. Complexity, opacity and confusion have their own political consequences. We return to this point in Chapter 7 below.

In conclusion, India's electricity system can be broadly considered a flat, two-storeyed pyramid: with generation, transmission and distribution being the base; and the regulatory commissions, supervising all three, being the second layer, framing their own policies and being governed by those imposed on them. We explore each part of the pyramid in the following four chapters, before coming back to the pyramid as a whole in Chapter 7.

Endnotes

1. Pargal and Banerjee, *More Power to India.*
2. Ibid.
3. Prayas, *Know the Electricity Act 2003* (Prayas Energy Research Group, n.d.), http://www.prayaspune.org.

4. Commonwealth Foundation, *Making It Flow: Learning from Commonwealth Experiences in Water and Electricity Provision* (Commonwealth Foundation, 2004).
5. Prayas Electricity Act.
6. The only exception the Act provides to this rule is for panchayats, cooperatives, consumer groups and other local bodies, which can undertake distribution without a license in areas notified as "rural" by the state government. At the time of writing, it is not clear if such notifications have actually been issued by any state government.

3
Generation

Perhaps the part of the electricity system that has seen the biggest transformation since the 2003 Act is generation. Two major changes have occurred. The first is a massive increase in generation capacity. In 1991, as discussed above, India had a total generation capacity of 69 gigawatts. As of December 2016, the country's total power generation capacity is 310 gigawatts—an increase of around four and a half times.[1] The second is the entry of private power generation companies on a large scale. Of the 310 GW of installed generation capacity, 42% is in the private sector (with central government and state government generation companies providing 24% and 33% respectively)—as compared to 3% in 2002.[2]

Much of this increase in generation, and particularly private sector generation, has been driven by the new models of pricing for electricity. Two primary methods are used to sell electricity from generating companies. The more common is what are known as "power purchase agreements" (PPAs). These are agreements between distribution companies and generation companies for the supply of electricity over a given period. Discoms are expected to make as many PPAs as they need to ensure that they have sufficient electricity supply for their customers, and PPAs are typically assumed to be the primary form of electricity purchase by discoms. PPAs are also notified to the regional and state level dispatch centres, and affect the manner in which these centres regulate the transmission network. The rate at which each generating station sells its power, for the purpose of PPAs, is set by the respective State Electricity Regulatory Commission after an application by the owner of the generating station.

In case a discom suddenly requires more electricity than it has prepared for in the form of PPAs, a different route is followed. Under the Electricity Act, as discussed in the preceding chapter, the discom can purchase power on what is known as the "merchant" or "spot" markets through licensed power traders. Some power plants (for instance, several plants owned by the Jindal corporation[3]) are set up entirely for the purpose of selling this kind of power, and the UPA government had originally proposed to have at least 12,000 megawatts in power generating capacity with merchant power plants by 2009.[4] Merchant power has both financial and technical implications—rates for merchant power are not regulated by the regulatory commissions, and it generally costs more than power obtained from PPAs (though this is not always the case[5]); and discoms are further required to pay additional charges to the dispatch centre in the form of "unscheduled interchange" fees. This is discussed further in the next chapter.

The massive transformation in generation is often cited as the prime indicator of the success of the 2003 Electricity Act.[6] As we saw in the first chapter, it has also effectively closed India's power deficit—though it has done so without necessarily remedying the problems in electricity supply in the country. Moreover, generation has brought in its train a set of new problems as well.

In this chapter, we first discuss each of the key forms of generation, and the issues that have arisen along with them. While each form of generation could be the subject of an entire book, here we are seeking only to elucidate their dynamics rather than describe them in detail. It is important to note that the problems that each form of generation has brought in its wake are not merely a question of bureaucrats not doing their jobs, or the fact that "there will always be a cost to any form of progress." Rather, these failures have a specific pattern, one that applies regardless of the form of generation being used. We return to this pattern in the section on regulation and perverse outcomes below.

1. Thermal Power Plants

India's largest form of electricity generation is through thermal power plants, where electricity is generated through the burning of fossil fuels—primarily coal, which as of December 2016 fuelled 60% of India's power generation capacity[7], but also natural gas and petroleum (8.2% and 0.3% of total power generating capacity respectively). Thermal power plants have a number of advantages as a source of electricity. They can be ramped up and slowed down on demand (unlike, for instance, most renewable sources of electricity), they provide a reliable continuous supply, and above all they are cheaper than most other sources—though the cost difference with some other forms of generation, such as solar, is falling rapidly. It should also be noted that the share of thermal power in India's total generation is slowly falling; in 2012, coal-fired thermal plants alone provided 66% of India's generation capacity.

But this is the, so to speak, electricity focused way of understanding thermal power. If we take a step back, thermal power has many more consequences than merely generating "cheap" and reliable power. Coal-fired plants require large quantities of coal, which in turn means expanding coal mines. As we saw in the introduction, if the targets for coal mining expansion set forth in 2011 were to be achieved, almost six lakh additional hectares of land would need to be mined. As of 2011, estimates already held that mining projects—with coal mining projects forming the bulk—had displaced more than 5 million people, most of whom had received no rehabilitation.[8] Moreover, both thermal power plants and coal mines are intensely polluting, producing massive quantities of ash, air pollution and toxic chemicals. Coal ash is now the single largest form of solid waste in China[9], and in 2010 it was estimated that the water requirements of India's planned expansion of coal-fired thermal power would require 7 billion cubic metres of water a year—roughly the same as the requirements of one-fifth of the population.[10]

In this sense, the idea that thermal power is "cheap" needs to take into account these other costs, which are integral to both the actual cost and the feasibility of India's electricity system. In the section below on regulation of generation, we return to how these costs are in fact not taken into account—with devastating results for people affected by these projects, for the projects themselves and for the electricity system as a whole.

2. Large Hydroelectric Power

India's classification of power sources separates hydroelectricity projects with a capacity of above 25 megawatts from smaller projects. The latter are classified as renewable energy, while projects over 25 megawatts are classed as hydropower more generally. Under this classification, as of December 2016, hydropower provides 13.9% of India's power generation capacity (down from an estimated 26% in 2007, as per the National Hydro Power Policy of 2008). As with thermal power, hydropower brings certain advantages, including the ability to ramp up production on demand (within limits).

But also as with thermal power, hydropower projects cannot only be looked at from the point of view of their impact on the electricity grid. The largest hydropower projects, and the majority of those built till the 1990s, are reservoir projects—dams that hold back a river, create a large reservoir, and generate power by releasing water from the reservoir and using its flow to drive turbines. Such projects submerge huge areas of land, again requiring the displacement of people and destroying riverine ecosystems that may be critical to the livelihoods and survival of people downstream. The resulting problems can at times affect millions of people. For instance, the South Asian Network for Dams, Rivers and People estimated in 2014 that if three dams planned on the Lohit, Siang and Subansiri rivers (in the North East) are planned, the downstream river flow would fluctuate by up to two to three metres every day—65 kilometres downstream. Moreover, projects are frequently planned without any attention to the dynamics of the river ecosystem, leading to problems like siltation and choking from weeds. Because of problems like these, as of 2009, 89% of India's hydroelectric projects were producing below capacity, and half of these were not even generating 50% of their planned capacity.[11]

In order to address these costs and risks, both government and private developers have largely switched away from large projects to what are known as "run of the river" projects. Instead of constructing dams that hold water in reservoirs, these projects involve diverting a river through canals or tunnels, where it then flows over (or falls on) turbines that generate power. In theory, such projects are meant to only divert part of the flow of water in a river, so that the river continues to flow and environmental damage is reduced. In practice, this is rarely the case. Like their larger counterparts, run of the river projects often involve bloated estimates of both river flow and power generation capacity. This results in both rivers running dry and projects shutting down. One of the largest such projects in the country, Nathpa-Jhakri on the Sutlej in Himachal Pradesh, has had to be shut down several times in the past due to lack of river flow[12]; and it has been predicted that if all the run of the river projects planned on the Sutlej are built, the river will essentially "disappear".[13] In Uttarakhand, the Comptroller and Auditor General stated that "physical verification of four out of five projects showed that river-beds downstream had almost dried up, the water flow was down to a trickle, and extremely inadequate for the sustenance of ecology and the local aquifers."[14]

Poorly designed hydropower projects can also bring more immediately devastating costs in their wake. In 2013, Uttarakhand was hit by terrible floods that, as per still unclear estimates, killed over 5,000 people. A Supreme Court-appointed "Expert Body" set up after the disaster found that two hydropower projects in particular had massively increased damage from the floods, in both cases because they had narrowed the rivers' channels and dumped waste in them. The Expert Body also recommended that 23 out of 24 projects they had been asked to review should be rejected. What eventually happened is discussed in the next section below.

3. Nuclear Power

Nuclear power represents a very small part of India's electricity supply—only 1.9% of generating capacity as of December 2016, and almost certainly a lower percentage of actual power generated. But it occupies a disproportionate part of the public debate around the electricity sector, particularly during the period of 2008-2010, when the then UPA government negotiated and secured the famous "nuclear deal" with the US.

Moreover, nuclear power is perhaps the best example of why a "siloed", electricity-only way of looking at power generation misses other major factors. Given that nuclear power is deemed a part of the national security establishment, nuclear plants are simultaneously insulated from most regulatory and public scrutiny and heavily promoted by bureaucrats and politicians alike. The results can be perverse. The Kudankulam nuclear power plant—discussed in more detail below—was pushed through on the grounds that it is vital to electricity supply in Tamil Nadu, but it not only did not comply with most applicable regulations, it has now completely failed to produce power on any consistent basis (it averages a plant load factor of approximately 25%[15]). A recent review of plans to put in place twelve nuclear reactors in two sites—Kovvada in Andhra Pradesh and Mithi Virdi in Gujarat—found that the estimated cost of electricity in both locations would be between three to five times more than current rates, and that the construction costs were likely to be several lakh crores.[16] Yet both are being pushed ahead in the face of local opposition, as Kudankulam was.

In such a context, questions arise as to how such decisions are made and why they are maintained in the face of contrary evidence. This is what we turn to in the next section, after first discussing the last form of power generation—renewable sources of electricity.

4. Renewable Energy

Over the last decade, the government has heavily pushed renewable sources of power. These include solar power, wind power, hydroelectric projects of under 25 megawatts capacity, and 'biomass generation' (essentially the burning of agricultural and other waste). As of December 2016, such projects accounted for 14.8% of India's power generation capacity.[17] As of 2014, wind energy constituted the largest share of such power production, accounting for 67% of generation among renewable sources; micro hydel projects accounted for 13% and solar for 7%.[18] Renewable energy is growing extremely rapidly—generation capacity grew at an annual rate of 22% between 2002 and 2012.[19]

The policy framework around renewable energy is considerably more complicated than around other forms of generation, as the government has been seeking to encourage its use. The National Electricity Policy and the Integrated Energy Policy both set out the encouragement of renewable energy as major policy goals. Further, the National Action Plan on Climate Change also set a target of generating at least 10% of India's power from renewable sources initially, with an increase of one percentage point every year. After coming to power in 2014, the BJP government then launched a mission to generate 100 gigawatts of power from solar sources by 2022 (this target appears very distant at present, considering that total solar power generation in early 2017 had only reached eight gigawatts[20]).

This incentivisation is done through a number of measures. Under the Electricity Act and the National Tariff Policy, regulatory commissions are empowered to impose "renewable purchase obligations" (RPOs) on distribution companies requiring them to purchase a minimum share of their electricity from renewable sources. Most SERCs have imposed separate solar and non-solar RPOs, and the National Tariff Policy also set a target of a minimum RPO of 3% by 2022 for solar alone. But as of 2014, most states had failed to meet their RPOs, and SERCs were mostly rolling over targets from year to year rather than imposing penalties for non-compliance.[21] Further, SERCs are also permitted to provide preferential rates to renewable energy producers, who can bid for and receive higher rates than other generation companies. These rates can then be indirectly subsidised by the government; the National Thermal Power Corporation (NTPC), for instance, frequently purchases solar power and "bundles" it with cheaper coal-fired power to make it affordable to discoms.[22] Current policies also require that renewable energy power plants be given "must run" status, meaning that power should be drawn from them at their maximum capacity whether it is needed or not.[23] Finally, renewable energy producers are also given a choice—they can sell their electricity at the preferential rates provided for them, or they can sell at the normal (lower) rates and separately issue "renewable energy certificates" (RECs) based on the quantity of energy they have generated. In turn, discoms that have failed to meet their RPOs can purchase RECs to make up the shortfall. However, given most states' failure to meet their obligations under RPOs, sale prices of RECs tend to be low.[24]

Renewable energy differs in one other way from the other three forms of power generation—all those three require large, centralised power plants that then distribute their power, by necessity, through the grid. Renewable energy sources, however, are much more amenable to decentralised, local production, and in that sense there is no need for them to supply their power only through the formal grid. This has given rise to a recurring debate over whether only grid-connected energy should be promoted. In practice, though, this is what the government has done. Even in its earlier form, for instance, both the UPA government's National Solar Mission and its successor under the BJP have prioritised grid-connected solar plants,[25] while as of 2013, 97% of all renewable energy in the country was grid-connected.[26] Given the transmission losses that are inevitably involved in transporting electricity over the national grid, forcing all renewable energy to be grid-connected is not a potential waste of the possibilities of local renewable energy and microgrids (an issue we return to in Chapter 8). Moreover, it also brings problems for the grid itself, a point we return to in the Chapter on transmission.

Given that renewable energy sources are far less polluting, much more sustainable, and much less destructive than non-renewable forms of generation, most commentators assume that renewable energy projects have no costs beyond the cost of generation. This assumption is also reflected in policy; most forms of renewable energy production are exempt from environmental clearance procedures (see next section). But this is not entirely the case. As with non-renewable power, renewable energy projects also require land and other resources—with costs from that use. For instance, in one well known case, a private wind energy firm named

Enercon secured the use of 339 acres of common lands near Kalpavalli in Andhra Pradesh. This patch was at the centre of 2,800 hectares of land that had been painstakingly restored over a period of twenty years by the local villagers, and tree cover and forest were improving in the area. But since the land was government revenue land, and wind energy does not require an environmental clearance, the community was not even informed when the land was handed over to Enercon. The tree cover nurtured over two decades was then quickly destroyed to make way for roads, construction and wind turbines, with implications for the livelihoods of hundreds of families (who had used fruit trees as a source of livelihood) and the water supply in the region.[27] The national solar mission indicates that 57,000 megawatts of its target of 100,000 megawatts should come from new "ground mounted" solar panels (with the remainder being from existing and rooftop solar installations). With the prioritisation of grid-connected centralised installations, these 'solar farms' are likely to require additional land, for which no estimates have as yet been made.[28] Finally, micro hydropower projects result in smaller-scale versions of the same problems that large hydroelectricity projects bring with them—including siltation, dumping of waste, destruction of agricultural land and draining rivers of water.[29]

In this sense, renewable sources also bring consequences that need to be considered. Environmental and social consequences are not the only costs that they impose. They also bring technical risks. The question, ultimately, is the same as with all other forms of generation—is the regulatory system capable of dealing with these costs? What kind of behaviour does it promote, and who benefits?

1. A Regulatory Framework That Promotes Wastage

In all forms of generation, there are certain patterns that keep repeating. We can broadly summarise them as follows.

The first is that there seem to be many projects that are planned on paper but never come into existence. In Chapter 1, we noted how hydropower projects in Arunachal Pradesh and thermal power plants in Chhattisgarh both seem to have been planned in much larger numbers than would ever be feasible. Similar examples abound. In Uttarakhand, the Comptroller and Auditor General found that, of 48 private hydroelectricity projects cleared between 1993 and 2006, only 10% had become operational by 2009.[30] This pattern repeats itself at the national scale. In an interview in 2012, the Director General of the Association of Power Producers (the association of private producers) stated that thermal power projects with a capacity of 65,000 megawatts were likely to turn into "bad assets" (i.e. not become operational).[31] Further, in the only comprehensive evaluation of environmental clearances that has been done, the Centre for Science and Environment found in 2011 that 267 thermal power plants with a total capacity of 2,17,794 MW were granted environmental clearance between 2007 and 2011—more than twice the total capacity of all the plants that had come up in India in the preceding 65 years.[32] It seems highly likely that most of these plants are never going to come up.

In individual examples, even more odd situations arise. In Chhattisgarh, a company signed an MoU and received state approvals for a thermal power plant project that would cost 1,000 crores—when the company itself was worth only 5 crores.[33] In Arunachal, a company that had run a microhydel project with a capacity of 5 megawatts was allotted projects with a capacity of 100 megawatts.[34] In Uttarakhand, a project that had been approved by the state government in 2001 subsequently changed the project site, the head height for the turbine, and even the river on which the project was planned—but was permitted to go ahead anyway.[35] It is transparently clear that none of these projects was ever going to come up in the form that they were planned.

Then there is the second pattern, which is generation projects that are approved, supported and financed, but then consistently underperform. We noted above that fully 89% of India's hydroelectricity projects were functioning under capacity in 2009.[36] It was also noted that nuclear power plants are being pushed through despite the fact that they will produce electricity that is far more expensive than would be affordable.[37] Siltation of hydroelectric dams leading to the dam rapidly becoming non-functional; thermal power plants that are unable to obtain the coal to run;[38] similar examples abound. One estimate says that, if India's thermal coal-fired plants could just increase their plant load factor from 58% to 70%, whatever remaining power deficit exists could be wiped out without a single new plant.[39]

That brings us to the third pattern—a generation paradigm that frequently has devastating social and wider impacts, but whose impacts are not addressed by regulation. Cases of this occurring are so numerous that it would be difficult to enumerate them here. There have been environmental impact assessment reports that reported no villages exist near a hydropower project when in fact several did.[40] In the case of the Kudankulam nuclear power plant, coastal regulation zone clearance was not even sought, and the Environment Ministry later permitted the plant to obtain clearance long after it had been constructed.[41] Moreover, in a detailed study of three hydropower projects in Uttarakhand, two of the authors of this book found that none of them had delivered the employment and other benefits that they had promised during the clearance process—and more importantly, the state agencies in question had neither the capacity nor the intention to verify any of these claims.[42] In 2011, more than one-third of coal mines were violating environmental rules, and many of those newly cleared were planned for areas that were already critically polluted.[43] And in perhaps the most glaring example, as we noted above, the Supreme Court-appointed

Expert Body had recommended that 23 out of 24 cleared projects in Uttarakhand should be cancelled after the floods there killed over 5,000 people; but till date not only have those projects not been cancelled, the central and state governments ensured that all would continue (with the effective support of the Supreme Court).[44]

Such devastation is not unique to power projects, of course. But it is the conjunction of all three patterns that needs explaining.

Indeed, taken together, these patterns should be grounds to seriously question anyone who argues that "easing" clearances, permissions, or finance for generation projects is necessary for "development." On the contrary, it appears that clearances and permissions are actually *too* easy at present—too many clearances are being given, and too much money being provided, to projects that either don't deliver or never come up at all. All of this is creating a spiral of bad loans, displaced communities, and resource wastage—as a fundamental property of India's current electricity system. Why is this occurring?

Large power plants typically have to negotiate four regulatory systems, broadly speaking, in order to come up—three concerned with natural resources, and the fourth with finance. The resource-related regulations are: land acquisition; environmental clearances; and forest clearances. Specific projects may also encounter additional resource-related regulations, such as the rules that apply to coal mining. Given the long gestation of most power plant projects and their high cost, most such projects then also have to approach the stock markets, banks or both for investment and/or credit, and hence have to also deal with the regulations that apply to such financing. While these regulations are separate and usually operate in parallel, they all share certain basic characteristics.

Till 2013 land acquisition—the use of government power to take over private individuals' land for "public purposes"—was conducted under the 1894 Land Acquisition Act, a British legislation. After 2013, this was replaced with a new and much more detailed legislation. However, both laws retained certain basic features. The decision on whether or not a particular project constitutes a "public purpose" for acquisition of land effectively lies with the bureaucracy (though the procedure is more detailed in the 2013 Act, it also states that any project that can be considered 'infrastructure' is automatically a public purpose). Once the declaration is made, those who would lose their land have an opportunity to raise objections (only one such opportunity existed in the old legislation; the 2013 Act has a multi-stage procedure). The 2013 Act also adds that, in case of acquisition for a purely private project, the consent of 70% of landowners would be required. However, note that the existence of multiple other land acquisition laws for specific projects—and the ambiguous status of those laws, since the 2013 Act exempts several of them from the application of its provisions—means that it is not difficult to bypass these requirements. Indeed, between January and June 2015, the central government acquired land for over 200 projects, but did not use the 2013 Act even once for this purpose.[45]

Environmental clearances are required for most industrial projects under the Environment Impact Assessment Notification, issued under the Environment Protection Act of 1986. While some power projects—particularly those in the renewable category—are exempt from environmental clearance, most power projects would be required to obtain a clearance before being permitted to operate. Under the law, a project proponent has to approach the Central Environment Ministry (or for smaller projects, a state authority) for clearance. They are then asked to hire a consultant to conduct an environment impact assessment (EIA). The report of this assessment is to be placed before a public hearing at the site. Objections and criticisms at the public hearing are recorded, and, along with the EIA report, submitted to an Expert Appraisal Committee (EAC) in the Environment Ministry (or at the state level; also note that there are different EACs for different types of projects). The EAC takes a view on whether to recommend the project for clearance or not, and the Environment Ministry makes the final decision.

Forest clearances operate under a parallel procedure. Under the 1980 Forest (Conservation) Act, any 'diversion' of forest land for a 'non-forest purpose' (i.e. any purpose other than afforestation or forest management) requires the permission of the central government (in practice the Environment Ministry). Not all power projects require forest land, but many, particularly coal mines and hydroelectric projects, often do. In this case, the project proponent first applies to the State Forest Department. The State FD then makes a proposal to the Environment Ministry, who dispatches an official from its regional office for a "site inspection." The report of this site inspection along with the proposal for diversion of forest land is placed before the Forest Advisory Committee, a mixed body including both a majority of forest officials and three independent experts. The committee then takes a view on the proposal and conveys its view to the Ministry, who decides whether to clear the project or not. After the passage of the Forest Rights Act in 2006, and an explicit order in 2009, an extra step was added to this process—at least on paper: the informed consent of the *gram sabhas*, or village assemblies, of all villages in the area also had to be taken, with a minimum quorum of 50%.

Notwithstanding their variations, all these systems have two common features. The first is that they are *project specific*. Clearances are granted to projects based on that particular project's claims. The *cumulative* impact of projects on land, forests or the environment is rarely considered—there is no institutional avenue for doing so. Moreover, the overall need for such projects is also not assessed in any cumulative or holistic fashion. Thus, every project claims that it should get the clearance based on the need of the country for electricity, but as discussed above, no one totals or adds up the cleared capacity to see if the targeted total has been met or, indeed, exceeded.

The second feature is that these systems are *centralised*, bureaucratic, and hence unaccountable. Decision-making happens primarily within the realm of the bureaucracy. Perhaps the best indicator of how important this centralisation is to the system as a whole is how strongly every space for public involvement or engagement is sabotaged, ignored or shut down. Public hearings for environment clearances are routinely farcical, with objections mostly ignored. The requirement for gram sabha consent under the Forest Rights Act has also been violated in almost all cases by both the UPA and the NDA governments.[46] There have also been systematic efforts to bypass this requirement entirely by amending government orders, most recently in January 2017.[47] Most famously, in 2015, the NDA government made a strong effort to ram through an amendment to the 2013 Land Acquisition Act in order to remove provisions for social impact assessment and landowners' consent. It failed to do so, but several state governments have passed these amendments at their level or are trying to do so.[48] The net result of such changes is that decisions can be made by bureaucrats without consulting anyone affected, and at times without even informing them.

Both these features have two consequences. First, contrary to what you might read in the business press, clearances are not a problem for companies. In fact, the exact opposite is true. Practically every project that seeks clearance or land under these laws is given it. Both environment clearance and forest clearance rates in India are in excess of 99%.[49] Conditions that are imposed as part of clearances are essentially forgotten, with less than one per cent being monitored for compliance.[50] In the previously mentioned study of three hydroelectric projects, some of the present authors found that the regulatory system had no way of even checking whether companies were meeting their commitments.[51]

In other words, the only characteristic that this clearance system rewards is a company or contractor's ability to be a "fixer"—to bribe, cajole or pressurise the right official at the right time, so that their clearance comes through quickly. This explains the regulatory failures around so many power projects, and the irrationality of clearing a far larger number of projects than is either required or feasible.

But there is one last piece of the puzzle—why do we have project proponents proposing projects that are unlikely to ever come up at all? How do they make money from a project that won't earn anything? That brings us to the financial regulatory system for such projects, which is as irrational as the natural resource one.

Power projects present a dangerous combination for an outside financier. As said, they typically require a large initial investment of money, and they often take several years to come up. But, at the same time, they are effectively guaranteed a minimum profit by the National Tariff Policy and the Electricity Act (15.5% "return on equity" is supposed to be ensured by regulators, according to the National Tariff Policy). Moreover, the entire policy environment, including the regulatory commissions, is geared towards ensuring that returns are not only maintained but risks are reduced. This point is discussed further in Chapter 6, where we discuss examples of how regulators have allowed generators to get away with overinvoicing, where fuel price changes have been allowed to be passed on to consumers (till very recently), and so on. Indeed, the central government's UDAY scheme (discussed further in Chapter 5) explicitly requires regulators to adjust prices every quarter to allow for changes in the price of fuel.

This combination of circumstances creates a massive incentive for financial institutions to lend money, and private investors to invest, on the grounds that they are effectively assured of profits by government policy. Few other businesses can offer any guarantee like that. But the long gestation period makes it possible for the project proponent to effectively trade on the *promise* of these future returns rather than on actually making money. This kind of trading on future promises is usually described as "speculation", and it is one of the central features of India's power sector. It is also one of the key reasons for the destructiveness and wastefulness that were discussed above.

There are several ways in which a promoter can profit from speculation. The easiest is to simply take loans from banks and then fail to repay them. Reserve Bank of India regulations permit "infrastructure" projects a number of concessions, and as a result such projects may be funded by loans up to 80% of their capital. The RBI does not require that banks verify that projects have obtained all the necessary clearances, and does not require any diligence to check if the project is likely to face local opposition. All this means that, for instance, a company that has secured a captive coal mine can simply start taking loans on the basis of likely future profits without any idea of whether it can ever operationalise that mine—or even without checking whether it could ever mortgage that mine in the first place. The CAG found a similar pattern at work in land acquisition in general (though this was outside the power sector); in Odisha, developers had secured 75,000 crores worth of loans on the basis of mortgaging acquired by the state,[52] and in a separate investigation it found that eleven companies out of a small sample of Special Economic Zone developers had mortgaged land acquired for SEZ purposes, for a total of 6,300 crores.[53]

Once the loan has been taken, non-repayment becomes the norm. Though India now has a bankruptcy law, this is a recent development, and it has not affected India's soaring bad loans crisis. Out of these bad loans, as per the Reserve Bank of India, the power sector accounted for the largest share in 2015.[54]. While the RBI data does not break this down further into bad loans to discoms and bad loans to generating companies, a World Bank report notes that of 2011, discoms accounted for only 36% of the bad loans to the sector.[55] The vast majority of the remainder would have gone to power companies. The exposure of banks to these projects in turn becomes a justification for clearing even more of them. Thus, in 2012, when overruling a rare rejection by the Forest Advisory Committee, then Environment Minister Jayanthi Natarajan specifically cited "huge exposure to nationalised banks" to ram through clearance for the controversial Mahan coal mine (meant to supply coal to two private sector thermal power plants, which had in turn been granted huge loans on the basis of their proposed captive coal mine—before it had obtained any clearance). Former RBI Governor Raghuram Rajan referred to this approach when he stated that "the system protects the large borrower and his divine right to stay in control."[56]

Similarly, where power generation projects draw on public investment or investors other than the promoter, it is easy for them to simply take in investment and then not deliver on the project (as with RBI regulations, SEBI regulations do not specifically require projects to publicly state risks from lack of clearance or community consent). Unsurprisingly, in a 2016 study on large stalled projects in India, power projects accounted for more than all other sectors combined out of the sample of 80 large stalled projects that fit the study's criteria.[57] Investors who invest in these projects have no way of recouping their investment, while the promoter has made money on the project.

The final way in which project promoters can make money on these projects is to obtain some clearances or mining leases, and then sell their entire company to someone else (on the promise of future profits based on these clearances). In 2012, BJP MP Hansraj Ahir alleged that such manoeuvres had ensured that over 50 captive coal blocks had been sold;[58] an *Economic Times* investigation found several examples of this practice.[59] As of 2013, not a single one of the 130 hydroelectric projects that had been allotted sites in Arunachal Pradesh between 2006 and 2009 had started production, and all were planning to sell their projects.[60]

We might note here that the biggest recent 'reform' in power projects in India—the shift from allotment to auctioning of coal mines—does not actually address any of these issues. The auctioned coal mines are still subject to the same regulatory system. Moreover, by auctioning the mines *prior* to the environmental and forest clearance processes, and without any regard for the fact that there is no longer any generation deficit, the government has created a vast constituency of large projects (with significant loans and investment secured) for mines that are possibly neither environmentally nor socially nor economically viable.[61] The sole advertised gain from these auctions was a supposed increase in government revenue, but this too is mostly notional at this point.[62]

In sum, what does all this mean? It means that, while there has been a huge expansion in power generation in India, this expansion has been massively distorted by two factors—the effectively guaranteed return on investment that the central government promises, and financial and resource regulatory systems that are highly centralised and unaccountable. This has created a system where underperformance and fraud are common; and where widespread destruction and injustice are pushed through in the name of development. Wastefulness and profiteering dominate the sector in a way that mere "improved generation statistics" mask. This problem, as we shall see, is a pattern throughout the electricity system.

Endnotes

1. Data drawn from the website of the Ministry of Power.
2. Prayas, *Know the Electricity Act 2003.*
3. Amritha Pillay, "Costly Imported Coal Squeeze Power Producers' Margins," *Business Standard* (n.d.).
4. Thillai Annamalai, "Merchant Power Plants in India: Risk Analysis Using Simulation," *International Journal of Energy Sector Management* (December 2009).
5. J.D. Kulkarni, "Business Landscape," *Power Watch India* (n.d.), http://powerwatchindia.com/business-landscape/.
6. See, for instance, Pargal and Banerjee, *More Power to India.*
7. Data from the website of the Ministry of Power.
8. Singh, "Presentation to National Consultation on Takeover of Common Lands."
9. Michael Lazarus and Chelsea Chandler, "Coal Power in the Cdm: Issues and Options" (Stockholm Environment Institute, November 2011).
10. Greenpeace, *Mining Impacts,* 11 April 2010, http://www.greenpeace.org/international/en/campaigns/climate-change/coal/Mining-impacts/.
11. Himanshu Thakkar, *There Is Little Hope Here: Critique on India's Climate Plan* (South Asian Network on Dams, Rivers; People, 2009).
12. Himachal Live Service, "Higher Silt Level Shuts Down SJVNL Power Project," *Himachal Times* (20 July 2010).
13. Manshi Asher, "Buying Silence, Manufacturing Consent," *InfochangeIndia.org* (20 December 2011), http://infochangeindia.org/water-resources/features/buying-silence-manufacturing-consent.html.
14. Comptroller and Auditor General, *Performance Audit of Hydropower Development Through Private Sector Participation* (Government of Uttarakhand, 31 March 2009).
15. Jayaraman and Kumar, "There is No Power Shortage in the Country—But the Entire Sector is in a Mess."
16. David Schlissel, *Bad Choice: The Risks, Costs and Viability of Proposed US Nuclear Reactors in India* (IEEFA, 30 March 2016).
17. Data from Ministry of Power website.
18. P.R. Krithika and S. Mahajan, *Background Paper on Governance of Renewable Energy in India: Issues and Challenges* (TERI, March 2014).
19. Ibid.
20. Kannan Kasturi, "Is the Government's Overly Aggressive Solar Thrust in Public Interest?" Journal, *Economic and Political Weekly* Vol. 52, Issue No. 6 (2017).
21. Krithika and Mahajan, *Background Paper on Governance of Renewable Energy in India.*
22. Kasturi, "Is the Government's Overly Aggressive Solar Thrust in Public Interest?"

23. Ibid.
24. Rita Roy Choudhury et al., *Delivering a Sustainable Financial System in India,* Inquiry Report (UNEP FICCI, April 2016).
25. Santosh M. Harish and Shuba V. Raghavan, "Redesigning the National Solar Mission for Rural India," *Economic and Political Weekly* (4 June 2011), Kasturi, "Is the Government's Overly Aggressive Solar Thrust in Public Interest?".
26. Krithika and Mahajan, *Background Paper on Governance of Renewable Energy in India.*
27. M Suchitra, "Green Energy Takes Toll on Green Cover," *Down to Earth* (3 October 2011).
28. Anubhuti Vishnoi, "Is Modi Government's Target to Increase Solar Power Capacity Five Fold in Seven Years Achievable?" *Economic Times* (22 August 2015).
29. Trepan Singh Chauhan and Shankar Gopalakrishnan, *The Fallacy of 'Balance' and the Irrationality of India's Resource Policies* (Social Research Collective, July 2015), http://srcindia.wordpress.com.
30. Comptroller and Auditor General, *Performance Audit of Hydropower Development Through Private Sector Participation.*
31. Rajshekhar, "Chhattisgarh Power Boom That Never Was."
32. CSE, "Thermal Power Plants" (Centre for Science and Environment, 22 September 2011), http://www.cseindia.org/userfiles/Thermal%20power%20plant.pdf.
33. Rajshekhar, "Chhattisgarh Power Boom That Never Was."
34. Rajshekhar, "Hydelgate."
35. Comptroller and Auditor General, *Performance Audit of Hydropower Development Through Private Sector Participation.*
36. Himanshu Thakkar, *There Is Little Hope Here.*
37. Schlissel, *Bad Choice;* Jayaraman and Kumar, "There is No Power Shortage in the Country—But the Entire Sector is in a Mess."
38. Rajshekhar, "Chhattisgarh Power Boom That Never Was."
39. Jayaraman and Kumar, "There is No Power Shortage in the Country—But the Entire Sector is in a Mess."
40. Chauhan and Gopalakrishnan, *The Fallacy of 'Balance' and the Irrationality of India's Resource Policies.*
41. Nityanand Jayaraman, "'Ex-Post Facto Prior Environmental Clearances': How a Nonsensical Phrase Was Used to Flout the Law," *Scroll.in* (11 July 2015).
42. Chauhan and Gopalakrishnan, *The Fallacy of 'Balance' and the Irrationality of India's Resource Policies.*
43. CSE, "Coal Mining."
44. Nitin Sethi, "PMO Meeting Changed NDA's Stance to Favour More Dams in Uttarakhand," *Business Standard* (12 March 2015).
45. Nidhi Sharma, "Not a Single Acquisition Under Land Ordinance for Developmental Projects in Six Months," *Economic Times* (30 July 2015).

46. Campaign for Survival and Dignity, "Bringing Back the British Raj in Forests," 15 September 2014, https://forestrightsact.com/2014/09/15/bringing-back-the-british-raj-in-forests/.
47. Nitin Sethi, "Changes in Tribal Rights and Green Rules 'Save' 130 Mines," *Business Standard* (18 January 2017).
48. Shruti Shrivastava, "Land Acquisition Legislation: Amid Central Logjam, States Move Forward," *Indian Express* (10 November 2015).
49. Kanchi Kohli et al., *Calling the Bluff: Revealing the State of Monitoring and Compliance of Environmental Clearance Conditions* (Kalpavriksh, 2009); Nitin Sethi, "As Forest Minister, Jairam Wasn't Anti-Industry," *Times of India*, 24 July 2011.
50. Kohli et al., *Calling the Bluff*.
51. Chauhan and Gopalakrishnan, *The Fallacy of 'Balance' and the Irrationality of India's Resource Policies*.
52. Supriya Sharma, "CAG Report Provides Hard Evidence Why the Land Acquisition Law Should Not Be Diluted," *Scroll.in* (17 July 2014).
53. CAG, *Performance of Special Economic Zones* (Comptroller and Auditor General, 2014), http://www.saiindia.gov.in/english/home/Our_Products/Audit_Report/Government_Wise/union_audit/recent_reports/union_performance/2014/INDT/Report_21/Report_21.html.
54. RBI, *Financial Stability Report*.
55. Pargal and Banerjee, *More Power to India*.
56. Raghuram Rajan, "Raghuram Rajan: Large Wilful Promoter Defaults Robs Taxpayers," *Business Standard* (27 November 2014).
57. Ashwini Chhatre, *Land Disputes and Stalled Investments in India* (Rights; Resources Initiative, 16 November 2016).
58. M Rajshekhar, "Over 50 Coal Blocks Allotted to Private Companies Have Been Sold: Hansraj Ahir," *Economic Times* (13 July 2012).
59. John Samuel Raja and M. Rajshekhar, "Coal Block Allocations: Private Profiteering from a Public Asset," *Economic Times* (7 August 2012).
60. Rajshekhar, "Hydelgate."
61. Rosencranz and Wadehra, "The Confusion Over Coal, Power Tells Us India Hasn't Outgrown the Need for Planning."
62. Nitin Sethi and Ishan Bakshi, "Government Claims of Windfall Gains from Coal Auction Lack Clarity," *Business Standard* (21 April 2015).

4
Transmission

Transmission of electricity in India is primarily handled through what is known as the National Grid. Initially, as electricity was a state subject, major states had separate grids (high voltage lines for transmission of electricity over distances). These were then interconnected into five regional grids—the North Eastern Grid, the Eastern Grid, the Northern Grid, the Western Grid and the Southern Grid. In 1991, the North Eastern and Eastern Grids were connected into a single grid. The Western Grid joined them over a decade later, in 2003, and the Northern Grid in 2006. Finally, in 2013, the Southern Grid was connected to the others, placing almost the entire territory of the country (with the exception of the Andaman and Nicobar Islands and the Lakshadweep Islands) on a single synchronous grid.

Unlike generation, transmission remains primarily in the hands of government entities. In this respect India is not unusual; indeed, it is one of the few countries in the world where transmission has been opened to private participation at all.[1] Transmission of electricity is often seen as a 'natural monopoly', since building multiple electricity networks would involve gigantic duplication of investment; and in this sense public sector entities would tend to take the lead. Despite this, as discussed below, both UPA and NDA governments have been pushing strongly for private sector involvement to increase, and many policies have been made with this purpose in mind. Despite this, as of 2014, the Power Grid Corporation of India Ltd. (PGCIL) controlled 80% of interstate transmission capacity, with the remainder largely owned by state government transmission companies.[2]

As we saw above, transmission is now often regarded as one of the major bottlenecks for electricity supply in India, with grid capacity having not kept up with increases in generation capacity. One estimate says that less than half the required transmission capacity has been added for every megawatt of generation capacity that has been added.[3] Another notes that, between 2008 and 2013, generation capacity grew by 50% but transmission capacity only increased by 30%.[4] The difference is particularly large in some regions; the state of Chhattisgarh, for instance, was expected to have a power generation capacity of 20,000 megawatts by the end of the Twelfth Five Year Plan, but would need only 3,000 megawatts internally and have only 7,000 megawatts worth of interstate transmission capacity to carry the rest.[5]

Whether this diagnosis—an underprovision of transmission capacity—is the correct way to think about the imbalance in the electricity sector is a difficult question, and one that we return to in Chapters 7 and 8 below. But policy choices under both the UPA and the NDA governments have assumed that this bottleneck must be opened, and since the expected investment levels exceed those that the public sector has planned, the way forward is to incentivise private investment. Thus the National Tariff Policy says that any transmission licensee should be guaranteed a profit of 16%, up to 2004, and a profit of 14% thereafter. In response to complaints from private sector entities that PGCIL continued to enjoy advantages because it could apply for tariffs on a cost plus basis (i.e. it could ask to be paid a rate that would allow it to cover its estimated costs plus a profit), in 2011 competitive bidding was made mandatory for every project except those that needed to be completed within the next one to three years. Other steps were taken to ensure a "level playing field" between the government entity and private investors.

On paper, these steps had the sought-for impact, and as of 2014, out of nineteen gigawatts of planned new transmission capacity, 78% was under the private sector.[6] But the system of resource and financial regulation for transmission projects is the same as that for generation projects. They, too, operate under the same project-specific, centralised, unaccountable and arbitrary regulatory regimes for land acquisition, forest clearance, environmental clearance and finance. Unlike generation, however, their projects often traverse long distances, requiring them to negotiate with the regulators multiple times. Given the arbitrariness of the regulatory system, each such negotiation offers more opportunities for corruption and lobbying. As a result, on an even worse level than generation, the system rewards fixers and lobbyists, on the one hand, and ensures that unrealistic projects are often cleared on the other.

Hence it is not surprising that as of 2013, out of ten private transmission projects that had been cleared, five were caught up in litigation, while the remainder faced issues with land acquisition, protests and forest clearances.[7] In this sense, pushing for more and more private investment is only likely to result in the transmission sector becoming caught up in speculation and corruption on an even grander scale than the generation sector.

These regulatory and capacity issues are only one of the two major problems facing the transmission sector, however. The other is the question of management of a giant network like the national grid. This brings a new set of issues around power, control and administration that also need to be engaged with.

The grid is currently managed through what are known as load dispatch centres (LDCs). There are thirty-three state LDCs, five regional LDCs, and a national LDC. The LDCs, as discussed in Chapter 2, are government entities whose orders are binding on all those putting in or drawing electricity from the grid. The LDCs' role is vital because of the nature of a large-scale synchronous grid like the national grid. Electricity is transmitted over long distances using alternating current, and the frequency of this alternation affects the ability of equipment to perform. If too much electricity is drawn from the grid, frequency can drop below the level required for the grid to operate, resulting in shutdowns and blackouts.

In order to discourage this, the load dispatch centres are empowered to impose two forms of fees. When a discom purchases power from the spot market (as opposed to a long-term power purchase agreement), it places a burden on the LDC to ensure that this power can be supplied without disrupting other existing arrangements. Such spot purchases are hence subject to the payment of an unscheduled interchange fee.[8] Secondly, the Central Electricity Regulatory Commission prescribes a frequency band, and all state LDCs are expected to ensure that the grid remains within this band. States that overdraw electricity—i.e. take out more power than they have previously tied up—will force the frequency below the minimum. They are then subjected to monetary penalties, but few states actually pay these penalties.[9] Indeed, in 2009, several state LDCs approached the Central Electricity Regulatory Commission against the decision of the national centre to impose fines on them for overdrawing power. In the case the state centres argued that, first, they could not be fined as they were not "persons", and secondly that they had in any case carried out their responsibilities by passing on the instructions of the national centre to the discoms. The CERC rejected both arguments and held that the SDLC was responsible for imposing load shedding on the discoms and ensuring that overdrawing at low frequencies did not occur.[10]

All of these problems came together in a 'perfect storm' on 30-31 July 2012, when, in what was called the largest blackout in world history, the Northern, Eastern and Northeastern Grids all failed simultaneously. The first day's blackout was officially triggered by the states of Haryana, UP and Punjab overdrawing from the grid simultaneously, resulting in main grid lines failing at 2:35 am on the morning of 30th July.[11] This was brought back on line within nine hours, but the grid now relied on power from the Eastern and the Northeastern Grids.[12] Unable to deal with the suddenly increased burden of power, connections between the grids collapsed at 1 pm on the following day, bringing down all three grids—Northern, Eastern and Northeastern—and depriving over 600 million people of electricity.

A subsequent enquiry report by the Ministry of Power identified the key vulnerability as being the fact that several transmission lines between the Western and Northern Grids had failed earlier, resulting in the entire connection being dependent on a single transmission line—the 400 kilowatt Bina-Gwalior line. This line dropped below the prescribed frequency and failed on the night of 30th July, triggering a disconnection between the two grids and overloading the Northern Grid, which collapsed. When it was brought on line, the Bina-Gwalior line failed again, but this time the power 'swing' (the main load) was located within the Eastern Grid. This triggered failures within the Eastern Grid, which isolated it from the Western and Northern Grids, and then resulted in a domino effect on the Northern and Northeastern Grids. The Western Grid did not come down as it had sufficient generation capacity.[13]

This technical failure resulted, of course, from management failures. First, on the day of the outages, the state LDCs did not implement directions from the National and Regional LDCs to regulate their power drawing, resulting in the outages.[14] But this management failure in turn reflected a deeper failure to anticipate what was going to happen. This was despite the fact that a drought that year had resulted in increased power demand in both UP and Punjab, and that the Bhakra dam, a major hydroelectric power plant in Punjab, was only 16% full as a result of previous overdrawing. This combination of circumstances meant that, in June, the Northern RLDC recorded that the grid was below minimum frequency for over 70% of the time. One commentator implicitly speculates that this situation effectively meant that the under frequency relays on the grid, which should have tripped, were switched off to ensure that power supply continued—and hence they failed to stop the grid-wide collapse on 30th and 31st July.[15] In its report, the enquiry committee did not pin responsibility on any single actor for these failures. Instead, it essentially argued that the grid required better integration between generation companies, dispatch centres and discoms, with automatic sensors to ensure both increased generation when required and automatic load shedding at the discom end when needed.[16]

These recommendations may be one reason that the grid has not failed since, but they also highlighted a fundamental problem of decision-making in the grid itself. No one entity is responsible for maintaining the grid as a whole. As a result, each actor on the grid responded to its own pressures. State LDCs, afraid of imposing excessive power cuts and facing a backlash in their states, did not respond to instructions from national and regional LDCs. Generation companies did not ramp up production when they should have. As we saw above, fears of cutting off important states may have led to the sensors at grid interchanges being turned off. Finally, pressure on the national government to restore the Northern Grid quickly on 30th July led to it being brought online before enough power plants were back up, leading to the overloading and second failure on the same day.

Taken together with the capacity shortage discussed earlier, all these patterns indicate a basic disconnect between the actual way the grid is managed and the technocratic way it is "supposed" to be managed. It is all very well for policy to mandate that overdrawing LDCs should be cut off, but this is not necessarily going to happen. UI fees and overdrawing penalties may disincentivise discoms and state LDCs, but they cannot prevent them from simply ignoring them. In this sense, the political realities of grid management—like those of power generation—are much more complex than the structure of the Electricity Act alone. In the process, they make possible both potential profiteering and, more importantly, system-wide failures for whom, effectively, no one is accountable. In a 2007 evaluation, for instance, one commentator notes:[17]

> The unbundling process in the power sector also has contributed significantly to the growing complexity in grid management. Competition has heightened the market pressure, forcing system to be operated closer to its physical limits. The number of utilities especially at the state level has also increased leading to increased difficulty in coordination during offline as well as in real time. The conflict of interests, unclear responsibilities, inconsistency of objectives, inadequacy of resources and legacy issues among these utilities often impair the collective performance of grid management.

Finally, it is important to note that these problems are likely to increase. There are two primary reasons for this. First, as discussed further in the next two chapters, discoms tend to rely on spot power more than they should—and this is likely to drive up the load on the grid, as a result of unscheduled interchanges increasing.

Secondly, the push to increase renewable power generation, and particularly solar power generation, does not seem to take into account the implications of such power generation for the grid. As we saw in the previous chapter, both the UPA and the NDA governments have effectively promoted only grid-connected renewable power (and done relatively far less to promote local or regional power generation). But grid management requires a mix of generation options that allow for production to be adjusted depending on load. Dispatch centres evaluate demand based on weekly estimates of power demand cycles (which vary over the course of a day—for instance, evenings typically experience higher demand—and a week), and communicate this to generation plants. At present, large hydroelectric power plants typically supply the additional power required at peak points, while coal-fired thermal power stations supply the 'baseload' power that remains throughout the day. When plants do not supply power, the dispatch centre has to resort to "load shedding", or power cuts.

But renewable power plants, unlike thermal and large hydroelectric power plants, often cannot be ramped up on demand, and have their own irregular cycles that depend on sunshine, wind levels or water flows. This requires the grid to have the "balancing" capacity to manage these fluctuating power sources and match them with fluctuating demand. In a recent article, Kannan Kasturi has closely examined what this will mean for the Indian grid.[18] He notes that balancing requires either storage capacity, to hold electricity for when it is needed, or other sources of power that can balance renewable power when the latter is not able to supply what is required. But the Indian grid has practically no storage capacity at present, and the policy requirement that renewable generators should be given a "must run" status means that balancing their power within a state grid becomes very problematic (a sudden surge in wind power can require cutting back demand from coal-fired plants, for instance, and Kasturi describes how this has led the Tamil Nadu government to land in litigation as a result of breaking its power purchase agreements with thermal power companies). While various policy initiatives are being taken to both encourage increased storage and to incentivise plants that provide "balancing" capacity, all this is being done without any clarity on how much capacity is needed and how long these projects will take to come online. In short, to use the terms we have been using here, the regulatory problems that plague generation are about to start plaguing balancing and storage as well.

In sum, all this means that the technical, regulatory and management problems affecting the national grid are likely to get worse in the days to come. The division of powers between authorities managing the grid is multi-layered and requires a high degree of coordination—which, as we have discussed here, is complex even at the purely technical level (and which will become more complex as more renewable power enters the system). This technical complexity is then overlaid with an institutional system that is centralised in power, while decentralised in accountability, and opaque and out of reach for most of those affected by it. Simple calculations of increasing generation capacity, on the one hand, and raising tariffs on the other are unlikely to address any of these problems. We return to them for a more detailed discussion in Chapter 7 below.

Endnotes

1. FICCI, *Power Transmission: The Real Bottleneck* (Federation of Indian Chambers of Commerce and Industry, 2013).
2. Pargal and Banerjee, *More Power to India.*
3. Jayaraman and Kumar, "There is No Power Shortage in the Country—But the Entire Sector is in a Mess."
4. FICCI, *Power Transmission.*
5. Ibid.
6. Pargal and Banerjee, *More Power to India.*
7. FICCI, *Power Transmission.*
8. Vivek Pandey, "Electricity Grid Management in India—An Overview," *Electrical India* 47, No. 11 (November 2007).

9. Utpal Bhaskar, "CERC Plans to Further Narrow Frequency Band for National Grid," *Mint* (30 July 2013).
10. Central Electricity Regulatory Commission, Adjudication Case 2009/1.
11. Uma Maheshwari Anandane, "India's Largest Blackout in History," *Powercuts. In* (4 October 2012), http://blog.powercuts.in/?p=28.
12. Sandip Sen, "How and Why the Indian Power Grid Collapsed," *Economic Times* (29 August 2012).
13. Ministry of Power, *Report of the Enquiry Committee on Grid Disturbance in the Northern Region on 30 July 2012* (Ministry of Power, 2012), http://powermin.nic.in/sites/default/files/uploads/GRID_ENQ_REP_16_8_12.pdf.
14. Ibid.
15. Sen, "How and Why the Indian Power Grid Collapsed."
16. Ministry of Power, *Report of the Enquiry Committee on Grid Disturbance in the Northern Region on 30 July 2012.*
17. Pandey, "Electricity Grid Management in India—An Overview."
18. Kasturi, "Is the Government's Overly Aggressive Solar Thrust in Public Interest?"

5

Distribution

The one part of the electricity system that almost everyone comes into contact with is the distribution network. As discussed, under the Electricity Act, this is handled by distribution companies (discoms). Much as it promised a sweeping transformation of electricity generation, the new institutional structure also promised a major change in the way that electricity was distributed. The Act implicitly sought to set in place a competitive regime, where multiple distribution licensees could coexist and an "open access" framework would make it possible for people to choose who would supply their electricity. The assumption was that this would lead to more reliable electricity supply, better customer service and a more robust distribution network.

Fourteen years later, the ground reality looks very different from what the Electricity Act ostensibly aimed to set up. In all states, distribution remains in the hands of the same institutions that it was in before the Electricity Act. The two states that have, or had, private distribution companies—Delhi and Odisha—had privatised distribution before the Act. Aside from these states, except for a handful of city-level private discoms or "distribution franchisees", all distribution continues to be done by agencies owned by the respective state governments. The difference is that these agencies are now no longer part of integrated State Electricity Boards and are instead independent public sector companies subject to the same regulatory framework that would apply to any private sector company that chose to become a distribution licensee. Open access has remained almost entirely unimplemented, except for consumers above one megawatt, and the policy framework on this front remains confused.

As discussed in Chapter 1, most of the criticism about the present electricity system has focused on these discoms. Almost all state discoms are now heavily in debt. In 2015, the total debt of state discoms was estimated to be around 5.5 lakh crores (though it should be noted that estimates of this seem to differ quite widely between sources), and they were estimated to being facing annual losses of around 3.8 lakh crores.[1] Such astronomical figures are the justification for a series of policy measures intended to ease the financial health of discoms, especially the central government's UDAY scheme, which we discuss at the end of this chapter.

But it is not always clear why discoms are in such a state. In order to clarify how discoms actually function, we undertook a closer examination of one discom in particular—the Uttarakhand Power Corporation Ltd, or UPCL. We sought to understand how an organisation like UPCL functions, particularly in financial terms. We then tied these findings to our field surveys of the experience of poor people in accessing electricity, which we discuss in the next section.

When the state of Uttarakhand was formed in 2000, the Uttar Pradesh Reorganization Act that was passed by Parliament empowered the new state government to create its own power company, which it did on 12 February, 2001. In April of that year the Uttar Pradesh Power Corporation Ltd. (UPPCL) transferred all assets and responsibilities for electricity distribution and transmission in the new state to UPCL. Following the passage of the Electricity Act in 2003, in March 2004 the state government divested UPCL of its rights, assets and liabilities relating to transmission and instead vested them in the newly formed Power Transmission Corporation of Uttaranchal Ltd. (PTCUL). Thereafter UPCL was only responsible for distribution in the state, and till date remains the sole distribution licenses in Uttarakhand.

All our interviewees agreed that the UPCL is doing relatively better than other discoms in the country. Though our survey findings did not bear out any major difference between UPCL and the discoms in the other states we investigated (Tamil Nadu and Delhi), it bears mention that both those states are relatively more 'developed' and in this sense UPCL's performance may well be better than that in other states of a similar economic level. Moreover, one major difference appears to be that UPCL is far less indebted than other discoms, with its debts running into deficits running slightly over a thousand crores rather than tens of thousands.[2]

Officially, UPCL makes a number of claims for its own performance. In its submission before the Uttarakhand Electricity Regulatory Commission last year, the company claimed that it had met 97% of power demand in the state and that average supply is between 22 and 24 hours. It then goes on to say that there are "no power cuts" in the state—an extraordinary claim that we return to below. Between 2002-2003 and 2014-2015, it says its transmission and distribution losses have been cut by 25 percentage points, from 43% to 18%. It also states that it is replacing mechanical metres with electrical ones, replacing defective ones, and otherwise improving the infrastructure in the state. On the basis of all of this, in 2016 it sought an increase in tariff of 24.96%.

Such a large hike would appear to be justified on the basis of the widespread critique that discoms are not charging high enough tariffs. But UPCL's accounts hid more than they revealed, and the Electricity Regulatory Commission finally approved a hike of only 5%. The details of the manner in which pricing was calculated are discussed in the next chapter, and provide a rather different story from what one might expect.

The full context behind some of UPCL's other claims also provide additional context for how distribution companies work on the ground. The "no power cuts" claim is a good place to start. This claim, which the Regulatory Commission does not contest in its order, appears to be based on the UERC's definition of the term "unscheduled / emergency outages". The Commission had earlier ruled that any power cut that occurred over more than a certain number of hours for over fifteen days, or if a high tension (i.e. industrial) consumer is supplied less than 18 hours of power on average in a month, such cuts will not be treated as "unscheduled / emergency outages" (and a penalty will be applied). In effect, UPCL appears to have declared that only cuts that fit these criteria are power cuts at all, and everything that could be called an "emergency outage" is not a power cut. Thus, as anyone living in Uttarakhand knows (and as our survey shows), power cuts certainly occur, but on paper these are not called power cuts. In this particular case, both the UPCL and the UERC are failing in their responsibility for regulating and enforcing norms for better electricity supply, as regulations specifically empower the Regulatory Commission to ensure better service quality. In the next Chapter we deal with more examples of this kind.

Moreover, UPCL's claims on losses turn out to be somewhat questionable. UPCL's data shows that over 20% of connections in the state have metres that were either unread or defective. The discom hence 'estimated' power usage on these connections—which may mean that it can adjust its losses accordingly. Its collection rates had also fallen from 98% to 95%. The Commission goes on to pick more holes in several of UPCL's calculations. In one instance it finds UPCL claiming that public lamps were on for "obnoxious" (the Commission's word, not ours) amounts of time; a public water works is recorded as having run for 72 hours a day (the commission calls this, in turn, a "mockery"); a significant amount of money was spent on subsidies and discounts for UPCL employees; and a range of other calculation errors and possibly deliberate cover-ups. In its finding in the 2016 tariff order, the Commission records that:

> This signifies that either proper load monitoring is not being carried out and the connections are released on lower contracted load or fictitious sales are booked to camouflage the losses because of which the consumption/kW is coming very high and average revenue/unit is working out to be even lower than the energy charges. In either case, UPCL's revenue is being suppressed and is being loaded on to other consumer categories. This also reflects towards the inadequate monitoring of sales and revenues at the distribution/circle/zonal/head office level of UPCL. In fact during the current proceedings UPCL was asked to submit the reasons and basis for the anomalies discussed above. UPCL in its reply merely submitted that it has taken strict measures for curbing the same and the Field Officers have been directed to avoid such kind of careless mistakes and be accountable for such kind of errors. UPCL further submitted that in order to avoid such errors in the future and to simplify the monitoring system, the corporate office has revised the formats and, accordingly, circulated them to the field offices.

However, other than recording its anger, the Commission took no further steps on any of these issues.

Moreover, interviews with UPCL staff showed another reality which is not reflected in either the company's claims or the regulatory commission's orders. A retired UPCL staff member and union leader, Ashok Sharma, noted that the company has frozen recruitment of Class 3 and Class 4 workers since 1980.[3] In the intervening 36 years, UPCL had not filled any of these vacancies with permanent staff. The result is a severe staff shortage. The company runs what are known as "bijli ghars", or electricity houses, on an area-wise basis, and the prescribed staff strength of a bijli ghar is 25-30 people. At present, these bijli ghars are often run by a staff of three or four people instead.

Who fills the gaps, then? Both in our surveys and in interviews, two methods emerged as the 'solution' employed in practice. First, given that Uttarakhand has a large number of ex-servicemen (who had earlier served in the armed forces), the State government had earlier set up an agency called Uttarakhand Purva Sainik Kalyan Nigam Ltd. (UPNL), who provides temporary staff to several government departments. UPCL appears to have hired many people from this agency, though we were not able to get exact figures. These staff—mostly young men—come in with no training, and UPCL permanent staff complain that they do not know basic safety regulations or the nature of the work, and have to effectively be trained on the job. They are also frequently transferred in and out. This imposes an additional burden on the more experienced staff and harms the effectiveness of the UPCL as a whole.

The second method is that local electricians, linesmen, and others start to effectively "hang around" the bijli ghar and do jobs that are within UPCL's purview. Though regulations prohibit anyone from touching UPCL lines and poles except UPCL staff, the local staff themselves connive with such workers as they are unable to manage the workload otherwise. These workers earn an income purely from the tips, commissions and bribes that are paid by customers. Naturally, their safety and training record is even poorer than that of the UPNL staff and they are effectively not under any formal supervision at all.

The existence of such people is perhaps why, in all our field surveys, a significant number of people reported that they had to pay bribes in order to obtain electricity connections. While we did not investigate the staffing situation in other public sector discoms, given that most State governments have been engaging in government-wide recruitment freezes over the past two decades, it would not be surprising if it is a problem in most states. But neither the regulatory commission nor UPCL appears to have any way to address the issue. While a hike in tariffs may be useful, on its own it does not address the problem of the staffing crunch, particularly as UPCL itself does not refer to this problem in its official submissions. In a sense, there is an irony in those pushing for privatisation of discoms on these grounds—in a sense UPCL is already being privatised, from the inside out.

Indeed, Ashok Sharma argued that these steps were all intended to cripple the public sector discom, with the eventual intention of privatising it. It is easy to dismiss these claims as "what all public sector unionists say", but in the circumstances, such a glib dismissal does not seem warranted. But it does point to a basic failure of the electricity system, one that we need to investigate further. Unsurprisingly, these problems become even more apparent when we look at what poor and working class people actually experience when they seek to access the electricity system.

1. The Experience of Actually Getting Electricity

As part of our study on the electricity system, the present authors conducted detailed field surveys in four areas: rural Uttarakhand (Bilangana block in Tehri Garhwal District), urban Uttarakhand (the city of Dehradun), semi-urban and rural Tamil Nadu (in villages near Gudalur, Nilgiris District), and in working class areas of Delhi. Our focus in all four areas was on poor and working class families. In rural Uttarakhand, we focused on small farmers and agricultural workers; in Dehradun and Delhi, on construction and domestic workers;

and in Tamil Nadu, on tea estate workers and small tea growers. We excluded any family with a four-wheeled vehicle or other large asset holdings (e.g. in rural areas, land above the average holding). In total, we interviewed 382 families across all four areas—50 households in the city of Dehradun, 101 households in Tamil Nadu, 100 households in Delhi, and 121 households in Tehri Garhwal district. These interviews were conducted across multiple visits and by researchers familiar, in all cases, with the areas and communities being surveyed in advance.

Households were chosen through a so-called "snowball" method, using families that knew each other and us, and did not follow a statistically random sampling method. Random sampling would haave required a much larger sample size to provide any statistically meaningful conclusions, that would have prevented more detailed discussions of problems that may not emerge in single one off interactions. These findings should hence not be taken as statistically rigorous reflections of the population as a whole but rather as qualitative indicators of what it is like to be a poor person using electricity in India.

Our objective was to examine the validity of some of the assumptions of the 'standard model' described in Chapter 1, and of the public debate around electricity in India in general. To recap, these assumptions include two basic points: that pilferage and thieving (implicitly by the poor) is a major reason for the continuing high rate of distribution losses among most discoms; and, second, that the changed structure of the electricity sector has made both prices and service delivery more transparent and more responsive.

What emerged from these surveys was, on the one hand, not surprising; and on the other hand surprising indeed, since it doesn't quite conform to either of these assumptions. There were evident differences between the four field areas. But despite this, there was also a surprisingly high level of commonality in our findings. Whether rural or urban, private or public discom, some features of the electricity system were almost uniform across the board.

First, electricity costs were a significant part of a family's monthly expenses. They constituted between 4%-6% of monthly income (in the case of Delhi, rising to 10% in some cases). This was true in Uttarakhand as well, where, as we saw, the discom claims to have the lowest rates in the country. In Delhi, survey participants also pointed out that the slab system followed by the discoms (where rates are raised for higher consumers) involved sharp jumps in tariff between slabs, meaning that if a user crossed the slab limit at any point, their rates increased manifold. Given all these facts, raising electricity costs sharply can have a significant impact on large numbers of poor people.

In addition, particularly in the rural areas we surveyed, payment of bills required travelling over long distances and frequently wasting a day (which involves the loss of wages for most daily wage and casual workers). Thus, in Tamil Nadu, some participants reported that the nearest bill payment office was eight kilometres away and the total time, including travel, to pay the bill added up to over three hours (which effectively meant losing the day as far as earning is concerned). In Uttarakhand, in our survey, the minimum distance was four kilometres and the maximum 25 kilometres.

Confirming earlier findings, we also found that electricity penetration—in the sense of having a connection—does not necessarily mean that people have been able to use all the devices that most middle or upper class households would take as a given. The two devices that practically every connected household had were lights and TVs. Only rural Uttarakhand was an exception to this pattern, with a significant proportion of households (18%) that had a connection but did not have a TV, and only one in six households reported using lights frequently (interestingly, this showed that many households had TVs but not lights). TVs are not a small investment—the price of one is roughly twice the median monthly income of the households we surveyed, except in the case of Delhi—but the sample confirmed how important they are in people's lives. But after lights and TVs, other 'basic' devices show a rapid drop off in usage. Fans, which are essential in most parts of the country in the summer, were by no means universal. Only in Delhi did every surveyed household have one. In Dehradun and in Tamil Nadu, approximately half had a fan; and in rural Uttarakhand the proportion dropped to one fourth. Apart from fans, basic cooking appliances showed a similar pattern. In Tamil Nadu, perhaps reflecting recent welfare schemes, penetration of mixers and grinders was almost universal, but in Delhi and rural Uttarakhand mixers were owned by barely one in ten households (indeed, Delhi reported no mixers). All the areas we surveyed also have cool to cold winters, but water heaters were similarly rare; one in three households in Tamil Nadu and Dehradun, and one in twenty in rural Uttarakhand.

This indicates that some factors in the present situation are still not sufficient for people to afford to use what many readers of this study would regard as basic amenities. Is it merely that people cannot afford these devices? While that is clearly a problem, other survey findings indicate that the electricity system itself might be responsible. First, in all our study areas, survey participants reported significant daily power cuts, generally for at least an hour a day (one should note however that this is far better than rural areas in most of the country, based on anecdotal evidence). The power cut situation was the worst in Tamil Nadu, with all participants reporting at least four hours of cuts in a day. Rural and urban Uttarakhand were far better, with the majority reporting power cuts of between one to two hours a day. Interestingly, Delhi, with its private discoms and better power supply situation, was in roughly the same situation as Uttarakhand; but many of our participants mentioned in passing that they work in wealthier areas of the city, and that there was a marked difference in the power cut situation between their slums and the wealthier areas. Such discrimination was not reported in our other urban survey (in Dehradun).

Further, voltage fluctuations and power surges are another major issue. These were most widely reported in Tamil Nadu. But in all four areas, people reported losing appliances as a result of problems in electricity supply. This was best in Delhi, where only four households (out of 100) reported losing TVs or other devices. In Tamil Nadu, however, almost one in six households had their TVs damaged by fluctuations, and one in five had mixers or grinders damaged; in Dehradun, similarly, one in six households reported losing some major appliance to problems in electricity supply. In Tamil Nadu and Dehradun another common complaint was loss of electricity metres (and, in Dehradun, mains connection wires). For a working class family, the loss of a TV or another major appliance (such as a mixer or, in one case, a refrigerator) is not a small loss, and the family may struggle to replace the device.

In this sense, the electricity system is still not good enough for poor and working class families to rely on it for continuous usage. But this takes us to the other question—how common is power theft? Are these households not receiving a regular supply because their connections are ad hoc or illegal?

This brings us to perhaps the most interesting finding of the survey—every household in our sample, in all four areas, that had electricity had a metreed, official connection. Keeping in mind the fact that people may not admit to having an illegal or stolen connection themselves, we then asked in the survey whether they were aware of any households (without needing to name any) that had stolen connections. In all four areas, all survey participants were clear that they did not know any such household. Indeed, in only one of our survey sites—Dehradun—did people refer to power theft in slums at all, and in that case, they said, theft occurs for short-term use (most of those surveyed reported that they had temporarily hooked up an illegal connection either when their house was being built—for tile polishing—or for a social event like a *jagran*, etc.). But such connections were typically disconnected in a day or two, and no household used stolen electricity on a regular basis. In Delhi, some participants referred to illegal consumption by industrial units in industrial areas, but not by households. While our survey is far too small for us to conclude that theft is not occurring, it is clearly far less widespread than casual references to "illegal pilferage in slums" imply. The stereotype of "slum dwellers" living on "stolen electricity and water" does not seem to have any resemblance to reality.

However, in such circumstances of low quality and irregular supply, was the regulatory machinery accessible to our survey participants? We found that the answer was no, as might be expected. Only in Delhi were our survey participants aware of the existence of the discoms' formal grievance redressal machinery or the regulatory commissions (though many were not aware of its official purpose). In Delhi, the complaint centres set up by the discoms were said to have a very poor response rate, especially in slum areas. Participants also complained that there are very few complaint centres and that registration of complaints involves long delays, after which the complaint itself is not attended to for long periods of time. In Uttarakhand and Tamil Nadu, our participants did not even know about the grievance redressal systems (such as Uttarakhand's Consumer Grievance Redressal Forum) and instead approached local discom officials for help. In Tamil Nadu, participants named the lineman, the bill clerk, and the assistant engineer as those whose help they most often sought. Since these had earlier been government officials, they were still perceived as such, and in Tamil Nadu the discom is still routinely referred to as the EB (Electricity Board); in Uttarakhand it is often called the "bijli vibhaag" (electricity department). In Tamil Nadu they noted that getting a complaint addressed took repeated visits.

Perhaps more important—and more interesting, considering that it was also reported in Delhi—was the fact that corruption was also an integral part of the electricity service system. In rural Uttarakhand and even in a small number of cases (five) in Delhi, participants reported that they had to pay bribes at the time of paying their bills. In all four areas they reported having to pay bribes for getting a connection. This was universal in Tamil Nadu and rural Uttarakhand. In Dehradun, 85% of households reported having to pay a bribe, while in Delhi 40% of households had to do so. The figure for Delhi is lower, but it is striking that even in an area managed by a private discom, bribes were taken for setting up connections. The amounts involved were not small; when asked by our researchers in Dehradun, survey participants reported paying even sums as large as Rs. 25,000 (though the median was around Rs. 2,000). Moreover, in all four areas, including in Delhi, participants reported that they had to pay bribes to get complaints resolved. Once again the percentage in Delhi was lower—approximately one-third of those who had complained reported having to pay a bribe—though many of the complaints for which bribes were not paid were not resolved.

All of this indicates that the distribution network is not working the way it is supposed for the majority of Indians. Our survey effectively found a combination of relatively high prices, poor service quality, corruption and, perhaps most importantly, lack of accountability, as the key characteristics of the experience of the electricity system for poor and working class people. This emerges as a sense of powerlessness and helplessness in the face of such an unreliable system (and, as a corollary, to massive popularity for any politician who credibly promises to address these issues). This is true even in Delhi, which is almost unique in the country in having highly organised interventions in the electricity regulatory system by consumer groups. But it is perhaps a confirmation of the fact that most of these groups represent middle and upper class consumers that their interventions do not seem to have reached those in our survey.

Together with the displacement and destruction wreaked by many generation projects, this experience indicates how *unjust* the country's electricity system presently is. We return to this perspective in Chapters 7 and 8 below.

2. Some Proposals for Improving Distribution

Aside from the question of raising tariffs, there are other key policy initiatives that are often discussed in the context of improving the distribution network. We touch upon three of the crucial ones here.

1. Proposed Amendment to Separate "Distribution" from "Supply"

In 2014, the NDA government introduced an amendment in Parliament that seeks to separate "distribution" and "supply", or "carriage" from "content", in the distribution network. In effect, this would introduce a new category of companies—"supply" licensees—who would use the wires, cables and other infrastructure of the distribution company, but which would be responsible to the final consumer for the supply of electricity. It appears that the Bill's intention is to make the discom essentially the equivalent of a transmission network, with the supply licensee handling the actual sale of electricity. However, the Bill also provides that there should be at least one government owned licensee in every area, and that one supply licensee—by implication, the public sector one—should be designated a "provider of last resort" that any customer can turn to as a supplier. The overall aim of this is that multiple supply licensees would compete for customers in the same area.

But the precise distinction between "supply" and "distribution" is confusing, and some of this confusion emerges in the discussions of the Parliamentary Standing Committee on Energy, which considered the Bill in May 2015.[4] The Committee noted that it is not clear who is responsible for which tasks, and that the supply licensee appears to have no responsibility for the maintenance of the distribution network. In such a situation, it would be easy for supply licensee to simply pass the buck to the distribution licensee for problems. A second concern, raised by electricity unions, several State governments and other commentators, has been that the supply licensee can "cherry pick" high paying consumers and leave it to the discom—the 'provider of last resort'—to supply poor consumers. This would worsen the already poor financial situation of discoms and make future network investments. The state of Kerala summed up all these concerns in its submission to the Standing Committee:

> The opinion of the state government of Kerala with regard to segregation of content and carriage is that it should not be made mandatory. There are two or four important reasons for it. One, it can never give a level playing ground especially looking from the perspective of the incumbent operator. The reason being, in Kerala, we have achieved 100 per cent electrification and 80 percentage of our consumers' base is domestic consumers. They are consuming 50 percentage of the power, giving us 30 percentage of the revenue. There are 4,000 SC/ST consumers who are giving us 30 percentage of the revenue. This is one area where cherry-picking can be done immediately... Regarding the concept of supplying licensee, what is the role of a supplying licensee? It is not very clear from this. As I understand, a supplying licensee's role is to

> provide supply of electricity, that is, he should have some PPAs (Power Purchase Agreements) with him, and he should bring the consumers. He has two important functions—having PPAs with him, and bringing the consumers. Now, if there is a problem with regard to the quality of supply, who is to be blamed? Is it the supplying licensee or the distribution licensee? ... It will create a problem between the supplying licensee and the distribution licensee. The supplying licensee will say that the quality problem is because of the distribution licensee and it will create a lot of litigation...While going for a tariff proposal, the tariff will be determined based upon the incumbent licensee's cost of operation. When the incumbent licensee's cost of operation itself is on the higherside, the new supplier who is coming in will be able to get power which is already contracted by the distribution licensee at lower rates and supply it to the high end consumers. It means that the incumbent licensee will bleed.

Overall, the supply licensee in this Bill appears to be nothing more than a glorified bill collection agency—but one that will be permitted to make profits by arbitraging differences in supply and consumer tariffs, without being responsible for any part of the network itself. It is not clear how this will improve the electricity network. On the contrary, it will add another step to an already complex supply chain, and increase the existing level of confusion, opacity and lack of accountability that is plaguing the supply chain already.

The Bill appears to have gone no further after the comments of the Standing Committee in 2015, and news reports in late 2015 implied that it had been shelved given that electricity demand is low in any case (and presumably therefore supply will not necessarily be a profitable activity).[5]

2. Separation of Agricultural and Household Feeders

A second proposal that has received a great deal of attention in recent years is the separation of "feeder" lines into separate feeders for agricultural and domestic purposes. These are the lines between the substation and the main power plants, essentially implying that two separate distribution networks would be set up. This would have two purposes: improving household supply by separating it from the potentially high seasonal demand of agricultural pumpsets; and improving accounts by making it possible to clearly separate (and limit) the quantity of free or subsidised electricity being provided for agricultural purposes.

This proposal became famous after it was implemented in Gujarat, where it was credited with greatly improving the domestic power situation. It also received considerable publicity as it was often cited during the electoral campaign of current Prime Minister Narendra Modi. As of 2013, seven states—Rajasthan, Andhra Pradesh, Haryana, Punjab, Karnataka, Maharashtra, and Madhya Pradesh—had either planned or implemented feeder segregation.[6]

A subsequent evaluation of feeder segregation in Gujarat and Rajasthan found that voltage fluctuations improved greatly in both states, but the impact on power cuts was less clear, particularly in Rajasthan.[7] Moreover, in both states, no separate metreing had been implemented on the agricultural feeders, so the accounting benefits were not obtained.

Will feeder segregation help? There seems to be a strong case that at the infrastructure level, in states with heavy agricultural loads (such as Haryana, Punjab, Tamil Nadu, etc.), such separation would be helpful. But it is costly—one estimate states that it cost 2.29 lakh per kilometre for 11 kilovolt lines in Gujarat—and amounts to a duplication of infrastructure.[8] Further, as we discussed above, it is clear that segregation of feeders is not the sole reason for supply problems, and is unlikely to address them in a major fashion in the absence of other changes.

3. The Central Government's UDAY Scheme

The final policy initiative is perhaps the biggest, and has been in operation since 2015. This is the central government's Ujjwal Discom Assurance Yojana (UDAY), intended to address the financial problems plaguing discoms.

The scheme relies on state governments taking over the debt of discoms by paying off their loans. This amounts to a bailout of the discom by the state government, and it takes the debt off of the discom's books. Since state governments can sell bonds to investors to pay for this debt, and state government bonds are usually at a lower rate of interest than the bank loans that the discoms had taken, there is a net saving of funds as well. So why can't state governments simply do this without a central government scheme? The reason is that a bailout would massively increase the debts on the books of state governments, and the resulting interest payments would place them in breach of their deficit limits under the Fiscal Responsibility and Budget Management Act.[9]

Hence, under UDAY, the Centre has essentially offered the state governments a carrot in the form of exemption from their limits under the FRBM Act for two years. In exchange, the state government would be obliged to take on 75% of its discom's debt—50% in 2015 and 25% in 2016—and to commit to covering 50% of any discom losses henceforth. The Centre also directed banks that discoms should be charged a maximum interest rate of 0.1% above the base bank rate.[10] Further, under the scheme, the Centre mandated that state governments should ensure that tariffs are revised every three months to take into account changes in the price of fuel; that annual tariff hikes take place; that unmetered connections should be metreed; and other steps classed as improvements in "operational efficiencies".[11] UDAY would be implemented by a tripartite agreement between the state government, its discom and the central government.

As of October 2016, sixteen states had signed agreements for this purpose under UDAY. Out of these, it was claimed, twelve had shown reductions in transmission and distribution losses; but two, Punjab and Karnataka, reported an increase in losses.[12] Some also showed marked reductions in costs, presumably as a result of their reduced interest burden; Uttar Pradesh claimed its costs had dropped had dropped by 50%.[13]

But, as with the proposed amendment to the Electricity Act, it is not clear what problem UDAY intends to address. This is not the first bailout of ailing discoms—two earlier bailouts took place in 2001 and 2012—and the earlier bailouts were not successful.[14] Out of the multiple causes of discom debt, which include poor financial management, poor purchase timing, and other forms of mismanagement, UDAY only addresses the tariff issue and provides a one time bailout on interest rates. More importantly, as we saw above and in the previous chapter, there are serious grounds for doubting that mere tariff hikes will address the problems that discoms are facing—as well as major grounds for fearing that they will cause great hardship. One calculation holds that Rajasthan and Uttar Pradesh would have to hike their tariffs by 30% to meet UDAY conditions in 2017 and 2018.[15] The impact of then revising tariffs every three months can only be imagined. Moreover, there is an inherent contradiction in stating that regulatory commissions should independently evaluate tariffs and then stating that a mandatory hike and fuel adjustment charge should be imposed. We discuss this contradiction further in the next chapter.

Such issues were taken up by some of the state governments that initially refused to join UDAY. Prominent among these was Tamil Nadu, whose Chief Minister J. Jayalalithaa publicly attacked the scheme during election campaigning in early 2016. She claimed that the scheme was intended only to benefit private generation companies, which were not able to sell their high priced power to the State discom; and UDAY would hence amount to an indirect taxpayer-funded bailout of private speculators and profiteers.[16] Given the nature of the generation sector, as discussed in Chapter 3, this criticism cannot be simply dismissed as election rhetoric. Further, in the AIADMK's election manifesto, the party also promised free electricity up to 100 units, which would have been barred by UDAY conditions.[17] After the AIADMK's sweeping election victory, in October 2016 the central government agreed to relax UDAY conditions for the state—it would not be required to mandatorily impose tariff hikes every quarter; its bonds would receive a five year interest rate moratorium, and it would receive a longer exemption under the FRBM Act.[18] After these concessions, Tamil Nadu joined the scheme. However, West Bengal, which also opposed the scheme on similar grounds, apparently has not yet agreed to any compromise.[19]

Endnotes

1. Asthana, "UDAY Is a Revival Plan for Discoms Rather Than a Bailout Package"; ET, "How UDAY is Going to Help Transform India's Power Distribution System."
2. Neeraj Sati, "Interview on Electricity Situation in Uttarakhand" (Secretary, Uttarakhand Electricity Regulatory Commission; Interview, April 2016).
3. Ashok Sharma, "Interview on Situation in UPCL" (State Secretary, All India Trade Unions Congress; retired UPCL staff member; Interview, 26 May 2016).
4. Standing Committee on Energy, *Report of the Standing Committee on Energy on the Electricity (Amendment) Bill, 2014* (Lok Sabha, 2015), http://164.100.47.193/lsscommittee/Energy/16_Energy_4.pdf.
5. Sanjay Datta, "Bill to Amend Electricity Act Put on Back Burner," *Times of India* (12 October 2015).
6. Ankur Paliwal, "Separate Power Feeders Can Greatly Improve Rural Electrification," *Down to Earth* (October 7 2013).
7. Ashish Khanna, *Lighting Rural India: Experience of Rural Load Segregation Schemes in States* (World Bank, 2013).
8. Paliwal, "Separate Power Feeders Can Greatly Improve Rural Electrification."
9. Neelkanth Mishra, "The UDAY Plug-in," *Indian Express* (17 March 2016).
10. ET, "How UDAY is Going to Help Transform India's Power Distribution System."
11. Asthana, "UDAY is a Revival Plan for Discoms Rather Than a Bailout Package."

12. Sarita Singh, "UDAY a Success: India's Power Distribution System Shows Clear Signs of Revival," *Economic Times* (3 October 2016); ET, "How UDAY is Going to Help Transform India's Power Distribution System."
13. ET, "How UDAY is Going to Help Transform India's Power Distribution System."
14. Shantanu Dixit and Ann Josey, "No Sunrise Just Yet," *Indian Express* (21 November 2015).
15. Ibid.
16. IANS, "UDAY Scheme Will Impact People Negatively—Jayalalitha," *Times of India* (11 April 2016).
17. Sanjiv Shankaran, "Jayalalitha Torpedoes Piyush Goyal's UDAY," *Business Standard* (6 May 2016).
18. T. Muruganandham, "Centre Blinks, Tamil Nadu to Join UDAY Scheme by Year End," *New Indian Express* (22 October 2016).
19. ET, "How UDAY is Going to Help Transform India's Power Distribution System."

6

The Regulatory Commissions

The heart of the post 2003 electricity system is the regulatory commissions, which are tasked with regulation of both pricing and of the system as a whole. Under Section 85 of the 2003 Act, the three members of each State Regulatory Commissions are to be chosen by a selection committee consisting of the Chief Justice of the State High Court, the Chief Secretary and the Chairperson of the Central Electricity Authority or the Central Electricity Regulatory Commission. Those chosen should be "persons of ability, integrity and standing who have adequate knowledge of, and have shown capacity in, dealing with problems relating to engineering, finance, commerce, economics, law or management" (Section 84). Both requirements—the selection committee and the qualifications—are waived if the state government wants to appoint someone who has been a judge of the High Court to the commission, though in that case the concurrence of the Chief Justice is required. The procedure for appointing the Central Electricity Regulatory Commission is similar.

It is notable that the selection committee under the Act does not include any political representative (in contrast to the committees for many other such statutory regulators, where the Chief Minister and the Leader of the Opposition are often represented). The apparent intention is to "insulate" the regulatory commission from the political leadership and the state executive and to make possible the appointment of "technocrats" who will understand the sector. This has been the logic for setting up such arrangements for regulators worldwide.

But while this may have been the intention, in practice, the vast majority of regulators in the country consist of bureaucrats. In the case of Uttarakhand, for instance the chairperson of the Uttarakhand Electricity Regulatory Commission at the time of writing is Subhash Kumar, an IAS officer who was earlier Chief Secretary of the State. This domination of bureaucrats is also nothing unusual, and applies to almost all tribunals and other 'independent' government bodies that operate in India. The exceptions for appointing judges also seem to be used very rarely, and indeed business groups complain that the Central Commission has never had a judge or a lawyer as either member or chair.[1] However, unlike some other tribunals and regulatory bodies, Electricity Regulatory Commissions are empowered to earn their own funds, and the Uttarakhand Electricity Regulatory Commission, for instance, aims to be financially independent of the government.[2]

As discussed in Chapter 2, the regulatory commission system assumes that the purpose of these commissions is to "balance" the interests of the "consumer" with the interest of generation, transmission and distribution companies for a "reasonable return on investment." This is implicitly based on the assumption that "balancing" like this will lead to a more accountable and more effective system of electricity supply.

At first glance, this looks very appealing, and it seems to make sense. But as we saw in the preceding chapters, in many ways the system is failing to meet those stated goals. Those failures are too numerous, and their character too closely related, for them to be dismissed as merely a question of 'lack of political will', 'regulatory errors', or even corruption. The more fundamental question is—what exactly are the regulators supposed to be balancing?

One half of the equation—the return on investment to companies—is easy to quantify, and a minimum return on investment has been incorporated in the National Tariff Policy. But the other half is not quite that easy. There is no one set of consumer interests. For starters, there is no one set of consumers, and their interests are not limited to just getting lower tariffs. Moreover, who is entitled to represent these diverse interests, and whoever they are, will they be strong enough, organised enough, and powerful enough to tackle the interests of organised commercial interests? If not, how can the regulator do any effective "balancing"?

In other words, the closer we look at the idea of a "neutral" regulator balancing two parties, the more the picture starts to fall apart. The final structural problem lies in the regulator itself, which is supposed to be 'independent' but which, as we noted above, seem to consist of retired government servants. Moreover, independence does not mean that the institution should be completely free of accountability—that would be a formula for corruption. In other countries, this problem is addressed by making the regulator answerable to Parliament or regional assemblies, in order to force at least a modicum of transparency and accountability on the regulators as well. But in India regulators are not required to report to any legislative body, and also cannot be summoned on the floor of Parliament. At most they can be called before Standing Committees and Parliamentary oversight committees, but the reports of these bodies are not binding on them (unlike in the case of Ministries). Regulators, in this sense, float in a kind of institutional limbo without any clear accountability to anyone.

The actual functioning of the regulators shows how these problems translate into practice. The primary function of the regulators is tariff-setting—fixing prices to be paid to generation companies and transmission and distribution licensees per unit of electricity. The manner in which these tariffs are calculated is regulated under the National Tariff

Policy, the Central Tariff Regulations (framed by the CERC) and each State Commission's own tariff policies and rules. The regulations provide for competitive bidding, especially in the case of generation tariffs, since distribution and transmission are controlled by government monopolies in most of the country (though, as we saw in Chapter 4 above, transmission tariffs are now also ostensibly based on competitive bidding). But in practice the Commissions are empowered to fix rates on a cost plus basis—that is, the company in question states its likely costs, and after reviewing these the Commission permits a rate that covers the company's costs and the rate of profit that it is entitled to. This form of tariff fixing is considerably more common, and the courts have also held that Commissions are entitled to fix cost plus tariffs rather than only ones based on competitive bidding. For generation, central and state policies provide that the generation company is entitled to recover both a "fixed cost" (money invested in equipment and infrastructure) and a "variable cost" for fuel. Transmission companies are entitled to only fixed cost. Distribution companies are entitled to their operational costs, the cost of power supply and their fixed costs; they apply each time with a "multi year tariff" application, that is meant to take into account both past costs and future revenues. Further, retail tariffs are set differently for different categories, such as residential users, commercial users, agricultural users, industrial users and the railways, and the Commission can add or subdivide categories further if it wishes.

But even with regulations that are very specific about the kinds of costs that will be allowed, the structure of the regulatory commissions itself makes abuses possible. We take three examples here, one from Delhi and two from the national level.

When evaluating the track record of discoms between 2009 and 2013, Kannan Kasturi found that, while their claimed costs continued to rise, Delhi's private discoms had barely reduced transmission and distribution losses and had not improved service.[3] Examining their applications to the regulator, it emerged that they were purchasing large quantities of spot power—that is, short-term power, through power traders, rather than through long-term power purchase agreements. The rates being paid also seemed to be well outside the norms. The Jindal company, for instance, had a plant that only supplied merchant power and a captive coal mining block to supply its plant; but though captive coal blocks were ostensibly allotted in order to reduce electricity prices, the Jindal plant was charging high rates. Moreover, the power trading companies handling these purchases were often the parent companies of the same discoms. After over purchasing power for a given period, the discoms would then allow that power to be sold back to power traders at much lower rates. This routine financial mismanagement was noticed by the regulatory commission, but instead of taking action, the regulator merely "gently chided" (as Kasturi puts it) the discoms and allowed them to pass through their costs to the consumer. In contrast, the public sector NDMC discom in Delhi managed its power so much better that it sold its surplus power at a profit and had enough long term power purchase agreements lined up to cover its needs. In this case, the regulatory commission had essentially failed in its role as a neutral tariff fixer, effectively taking the side of the private discoms.

A much more glaring example of this kind of action on the part of regulators—and, it should be noted, most commentators in the business media—emerged in the case of Tata Power and Adani Power, both of whom were operating power plants in Gujarat. In 2012, these groups approached the Central Electricity Regulatory Commission for a revision of the tariff they had been allowed under power purchasing agreements. These groups had received their tariffs through a competitive bidding process, and the agreements they had signed permitted any change in tariff only if there is either a change in law, or if there was *force majeure* (a legal term that means an unforeseeable event that delays or prevents someone from fulfilling a contract). In this case, the groups argued that Indonesian coal, the main source of coal for their power plants, had increased in cost due to a change in Indonesian regulations, and that they should be allowed to charge a higher tariff to recover these higher costs. This position was transparently illogical for two reasons—any private producer has to take into account fluctuations in fuel prices before making a bid, and bear the losses if their calculations fail. More importantly, in this case, the Indonesian companies selling the coal to Tata Power and Adani were either partly or fully owned by those companies themselves.[4] The change was due to the fact that the Indonesian government had directed that coal exporting companies in the country should charge the full rate for coal they were exporting, even if they were exporting it to their own parent companies. In effect, the only change that Tata and Adani were experiencing was a redistribution of revenues within their own companies.

The CERC, however, took the position that while there was neither a change of law nor *force majeure*, the companies should be allowed a "mutually agreed compensatory tariff" anyway.[5] The committee that fixed the compensatory tariff included representatives of Tata and Adani among its members, though they did not sign the final report; and the tariff that they awarded the two companies would effectively increase their revenues by over 10,000 crores.[6] A retired CERC official later justified the Commission's stance by saying that "you cannot run a power plant making monthly losses".[7] Following the CERC's order, the Maharashtra Electricity Regulatory Commission and some other bodies took a similar stand on applications by these groups. The energy sector NGO Prayas and some others appealed against the CERC's orders to the Appellate Tribunal on Electricity. In April 2016, the Appellate

Tribunal struck down the CERC's order, saying that the power purchasing agreement did not permit any such "compensatory tariff".[8] But even as it did so, it held that the change in Indonesian regulations could be considered *force majeure* and hence the generation companies could be given higher rates under that provision. It sent the case back to the CERC, which once again ruled in December 2016 that the companies were entitled to a higher tariff.[9]

Once again, the regulators here appear to have failed to carry out any balancing, and instead allowed generation companies to effectively milk the system to increase their own profits. Our third and final example shows what occurs when such systemic possibilities—that is, the opportunity to inflate costs—are exploited to the maximum—in this case, by the same companies.

In early 2016, it emerged that the Directorate of Revenue Intelligence (DRI), an agency of the Enforcement Directorate, was investigating over 40 generation companies for "overinvoicing" their imports of coal for power generation—with the amounts in question being approximately 29,000 crores. Overinvoicing here meant effectively lying about the price they were actually paying for coal. Both private and public sector companies were accused of doing this, and among the private sector companies accused of overinvoicing were Adani (once again), Essar and the Anil Dhirubhai Ambani Group.[10] The DRI claimed that in some cases coal was being invoiced for double the standard market rate (even if transport was included). Neither the State nor the Central Electricity Regulatory Commissions had questioned these costs, despite the fact that market rates are publicly known, and that the CERC at least had received a draft of the DRI's report.[11] Moreover, on top of this, in 2014 the DRI had initiated an investigation into the Adani group specifically after it emerged that the latter had overinvoiced the cost of equipment it was using in its power plants—with this overinvoicing amounting to over Rs. 6,000 crores. All these factors—inflated coal costs, inflated equipment costs, and 'compensatory' tariffs for events that would not actually have harmed the generation companies—would have been factored into the retail tariffs being set by the regulators, meaning that consumers are allegedly paying these companies almost 50,000 crores more than they should.[12]

In this last example, one might object that the regulatory commissions do not have the investigative machinery to look into details like overinvoicing. Indeed, they do not even appear to be able to settle the cases already pending before them. In January 2015, there were 734 cases pending before the CERC, and despite the fact that it is mandated to settle matters within 90 days, it was then considering matters that dated from 2013 or earlier.[13] In that case, scandals like this are not surprising.

But this example overlooks the fact that the basic premise of the entire electricity system under the 2003 Act is that the regulators will play precisely this role—or that some nebulous "consumer voice" will raise these issues before them. Here we see that not only were consumer voices unable to make a difference, even investigation reports from the DRI were ignored. This is not a reflection of the individuals sitting in these bodies—it is a reflection of a systemic failure, an expectation that an institution would be able to play a 'neutral' role when neither the capacity, intention or accountability for such a role exist.

Nor are such problems limited to regulators' relationship with private companies. We sought to study the functioning of one regulator in particular—the Uttarakhand Electricity Regulatory Commission—more closely, in order to see how a regulatory agency functions in a state with only one public sector discom, and in a state where consumer interests are not as organised as they are in Delhi or Maharashtra (from where most of the existing literature on the regulatory commissions has emerged). For this purpose we interviewed officials at the UERC and went through recent orders, rules and notifications of the commission. What we found was that, even when a regulatory commission is doing a 'good' job at present, the manner in which it is doing that job bears no resemblance to the model role that it is supposed to be playing.

The UERC was set up in 2002 under the Electricity Regulatory Commissions Act, 1998, and was continued after the passage of the 2003 Act. It currently has two members—the Chairperson, Subhash Kumar, who as mentioned earlier is a former Chief Secretary of the State; and Mr. K.P. Singh, from the Central Power Engineering Services, who functions as a technical member. The UERC claims to be financially autonomous, raising its funds from penalties, licensing fees and commissions on tariffs.[14]

The UERC's two main tasks are fixing retail tariffs for UPCL, the State discom, and generation tariffs for the numerous private and public sector generating projects in the state. In its detailed order—over 360 pages long—on UPCL's Multi Year Tariff application in 2016, the commission effectively rejected UPCL's attempt to secure a 25% tariff hike.[15] As we saw in the last chapter, the commission eventually only ordered a 5% hike. This major difference came down to the fact that the Commission estimated that UPCL required an increase in annual revenue of only 249.56 crores, whereas UPCL had estimated that it required an increase in annual revenue of 1220 crores.

The reason for the sharp difference in these estimates primarily came down to three factors. The largest was effectively an accounting question. UPCL had "banked" power in 2014-2015, purchasing power from a generation company with the promise of returning this (as electricity) in the following year. It had then effectively double booked this expense, claiming it both in the year in which it had received the electricity and in the year that it had to purchase additional electricity in order to return the banked amount. The UERC rejected this and held that UPCL could not claim this expense. This resulted in a drop of revenue required of over 300 crores. Secondly, UPCL had attempted to claim a "return on equity" even on money that was simply being held. The Commission rejected this as well and held that the company was only entitled to the guaranteed rate of return on money that had actually been invested. Finally, the Commission also held that UPCL was responsible for still failing to meet the Commission's standards on acceptable transmission and distribution losses, and deducted the amount being lost from the revenue required. In addition, UPCL was denied various other amounts it had claimed, such as interest payments and penalties on loans that it had mismanaged. All these decisions together led to the Commission's final order.

On the one hand, given the detail and rigour of the UERC's order, it certainly appears that the regulator is doing its job. Almost every claim by UPCL is examined in considerable detail, and the Commission lays out its logic for rejecting or accepting each claim. The Secretary of the Commission also informed us that the Commission had consistently tried to hold UPCL accountable for poor financial management and that they were very critical of the discom for not taking advantage of available Central financial schemes.[16] The same level of depth is visible in the Commission's other orders.

But what was striking was that *none* of these changes were made based on any input from the public. Indeed, a review of the manner in which the UERC interacts with the public reveals a very interesting pattern.

First, the UERC receives and records a number of public submissions during the tariff finalisation process. The majority did not raise precise issues on UPCL's claim but instead asked for concessions on tariffs to various groups or in general;

and the UERC's stock response to all of these submissions, as recorded in its order, was that it had not accepted UPCL's claims for a tariff hike. One group of submissions sought to challenge categorisations of customers, the Commission responded with a general ruling that it would not be "appropriate to disturb the existing categorisation." Moreover, a number of industry bodies raised specific objections to UPCL's tariff calculations. But it does not appear that the UERC used these either.

A second avenue of public input is the grievance redressal process, which is conducted through a Consumer Grievance Redressal Forum (CGRF). The UERC keeps track of the CGRF's functioning, and indeed we were told that they are aware that a majority of cases have been settled in favour of complainants since the CGRF was set up.[17] The UERC also issues a citizens' charter laying out the rights of electricity consumers. But in our survey we found that very few of these commitments—especially those relating to setting up new connections and repairing faults—were actually being met, in either the rural survey site or in the city. Moreover, the state has only two CGRF offices—one for Garhwal and one for Kumaon—which are thus basically inaccessible to the majority of people in the state. None of our survey participants in either the city or the rural areas were even aware of these forums.

Finally, the Commission holds public hearings. Unlike most regulatory commissions, UERC has gone beyond the statutory mandatory hearings and instead also held public hearings outside its premises. It has specifically tried to hold such hearings across the state. Prior to reaching its ruling in April 2016, it conducted public hearings in four locations—Pithoragarh, Sitaraganj, Pauri Garhwal and Dehradun. It also conducted the more routine mandatory public hearing exercises before deciding tariff changes for generation and other policy decisions. The public hearings outside the UERC offices had an interesting record. In none has the UERC recorded any submission relating to UPCL's tariff claims or calculations. Instead, those present at the hearing appear to have treated the commission as if it was a government department. For instance, in Pithoragarh, complaints were made that metres were being hung in unsafe locations where they were damaged easily; the Commission directed the Executive Engineer to fix this. The Commission also addressed issues like the provision of temporary connections without adequately checking if the transformer could bear the load (raised in Pauri Garhwal) and the failure to pay for street lamps (also in Pauri Garhwal).

This way of looking at the UERC was not confined to the general public. Even generation companies seemed to treat the UERC more as a representative of the government then as a regulatory body. In one public hearing the Bhilangana Hydropower Company (running a small hydropower project in Tehri Garhwal district) recorded its objection to the imposition of water tax on renewable energy producers, especially those selling merchant power, like itself. The Commission responded that this matter was out of its purview. Similarly, two industrial consumers objected to the imposition of a "green cess" on power charges, which also was not in the Commission's purview.

We saw an even clearer example of this process at one of the public hearings that we attended, in this case a public hearing on fixing generation tariffs that was held in Dehradun. This was a mandatory public hearing, to be held for decisions to be made on tariffs under the rules. Other than the researchers, no members of the public were present in this 'public' hearing. The only people present were the representatives of a private generating company and officers of several government departments, including the Uttarakhand Jal Vidyut Nigam Ltd. (the hydroelectric power arm of the state government), the Uttarakhand Renewable Energy Development

Agency (UREDA), and the State Industrial Development Corporation of Uttaranchal (SIDCUL).

Following an initial discussion about UJVNL's attempts to produce solar power on canal banks, the hearing moved on to an application by a private generation company called BSR Greens, which was proposing to generate power from waste incineration. BSR Greens wanted a preferential tariff of Rs. 12 per unit—well above the CERC's recommended rate of Rs. 7 per unit for incinerator-based power. SIDCUL, on whose land the plant was to be situated, supported the request. When asked why they should be entitled to this higher rate, BSR Greens stated that their technology is exceptionally clean, India has 13 of the world's 20 dirtiest cities, and waste elimination technology should be encouraged. A representative of the state's urban development department also stood to support the higher rate, though he seemed to have little idea of what the purpose of the hearing was. After listening to this for some time the UERC Chairperson gently intervened to ask how any of this was relevant to the tariff fixing process, which operates on the basis of well laid out parameters and not on the basis of policy questions like whether India has dirty cities or not. BSR Greens' only response to this question was that their capital costs are very high. The UREDA representative then spoke, and unlike the other departments present, opposed the demand strongly. He said this was untested technology, that if SIDCUL wished to promote it it should give up the royalty it would be charging for use of its land, and that the state urban development department was also free to subsidise the company if it felt that this was a technology worth promoting. But there was no ground for granting a higher tariff. The Commission then deferred the matter.

Thus in all these experiences of 'public input', certain patterns emerge.

First, almost no one outside the Commission—including generation companies like BSR Green and high tension consumers, both of whom might be expected to know the law—engaged with the regulator as a tariff-fixing body. Instead, as we noted above, all of them engaged with it as if it is a representative of the government.

Second, the "public" in the sense of 'ordinary' consumers was barely represented in these processes, and where it was represented its inputs were either not relevant to the Commission's process or were ignored. As we noted above, industrial bodies' inputs also did not enter into the Commission's calculations.

Third, where the Commission has in fact done a 'good' job, such as the scrutiny of UPCL's tariff claim or the BSR Green application, it has done so on the basis of inputs internal either to itself or to the government as a whole (UREDA's inputs in the latter case).

None of this conforms to the model that the regulatory system is supposed to follow. It is vital to not simply dismiss these phenomena as the result of public ignorance, lack of understanding or a lack of interest on the part of the Commission (indeed, in this case the Commission went well beyond what it was required to do). We noted above that the regulatory system assumes the existence of a "public interest" that is, implicitly, represented by an organised public voice that is then 'balanced' against that of the distribution / transmission licensee or the generation company. But there was no "voice of the public interest" visible anywhere here that was engaging with the regulatory commission. Rather, the commission functioned as merely another arm of the government—engaging with stakeholders, reaching its own conclusions based on internal data and findings, and so on. Aside from Uttarakhand, one might further note that even where groups that could credibly claim to represent such a voice attempted to intervene against compensatory tariffs in the Adani/Tata cases, they faced a sharply uphill battle and eventually lost.

In this sense, the extremely complex and detailed process under the Electricity Act might be held to have, at some level, increased the transparency of some decisions (such as tariff fixing). But it has not created any genuine process of accountable or 'balanced' decision-making. Meanwhile, it has also increased the opacity of the regulatory system and contributed to everyone from BSR Green to residents of Pithoragarh being confused as to what the actual purpose of the regulatory commission is. Moreover, in the name of independence, the regulatory commissions have been insulated from the mechanisms of accountability that apply to other government departments. All this creates a perverse situation where they are more, rather than less, vulnerable to being 'captured' by more powerful forces—even as the entire system and the policy discourse denies that any such thing is possible.

Endnotes

1. Shreya Jai, "The Trouble with Electricity Regulator," *Business Standard* (8 March 2015).
2. Sati, "Interview on Electricity Situation in Uttarakhand."
3. Kannan Kasturi, "Pricing Electricity in Delhi," *Economic and Political Weekly* Vol. 48, Issue No. 1 (5 January 2013).
4. Paranjoy Guha Thakurta, "Power Tariff Scam Gets Bigger at Rs 50,000 Crore," Journal, *Economic and Political Weekly* Vol. 51, Issue No. 20 (2016).
5. Ashwini Chitnis and Shantanu Dixit, "It's Time to End the 'Bid Low, Raise Prices Later' Strategy of Power Sector Players," *The Wire* (27 April 2016).
6. Thakurta, "Power Tariff Scam Gets Bigger at Rs. 50,000 Crore."
7. Maulik Madhu, "'Cheaper Electricity Is Not That Easy'," *The Hindu* (10 July 2016).
8. Chitnis and Dixit, "It's Time to End the 'Bid Low, Raise Prices Later' Strategy of Power Sector Players."
9. Shreeja Sen and Shailaja Sharma, "CERC Allows Tata Power, Adani Power to Pass Through High Cost," *Mint* (8 December 2016).
10. Paranjoy Guha Thakurta, "How Over-Invoicing of Imported Coal Has Increased Power Tariffs," Journal, *Economic and Political Weekly* Vol. 51, Issue No. 15 (2016).

11. Thakurta, "Power Tariff Scam Gets Bigger at Rs 50,000 Crore."
12. Ibid.
13. Jai, "The Trouble with Electricity Regulator."
14. Sati, "Interview on Electricity Situation in Uttarakhand"; Subhash Kumar, "Interview on the UERC and the Power Situation in Uttarakhand" (Chairperson, Uttarakhand Electricity Regulatory Commission; Interview, April 2016).
15. UERC, *Order on Approval of Business Plan and Multi Year Tariff Petition for Uttarakhand Power Corporation Ltd. for Second Control Period (Fy 2016-2017 to Fy 2018-2019)* (Uttarakhand Electricity Regulatory Commission, 5 April 2016).
16. Sati, "Interview on Electricity Situation in Uttarakhand."
17. Ibid.

7

The Realities of the Electricity Sector

As discussed in Chapter 1, our approach in this book has been to look at the electricity sector as a *system of provision* rather than purely from a technical or financial point of view. Our key question has been one of understanding how power (in the political, not electrical, sense) is distributed throughout the system, and who benefits at each stage from this structure. While the answers are diverse and complicated, there are certain common features—or, more accurately, common *tendencies*—that come across as a whole. In this Chapter we look at what those are.

1. An Opaque Structure and Dispersed Responsibility

One point that has come up in all three stages of the electricity system is the sheer *opacity* of the structure. This is not only because electricity is, naturally, a technically complex system. Rather, the system is opaque because responsibility is highly dispersed. As a result, the system is not at all transparent to those who are affected by its decisions—above all those affected by decisions relating to generation, and those relating to pricing and supply.

This conclusion is ironic, since one of the purposes of the 2003 Act was to replace what was described as an arbitrary, bureaucratic and corrupt system with a transparent and accountable one. But it was never very clear *who* it should be transparent to. From the narrow point of view of tariff fixing and official documentation, transparency has indeed increased. But from the larger perspective of allowing the system to be held accountable by those it is meant to serve, the result has been the opposite. Responsibility and power have been dispersed among so many different authorities and with so much complexity that the structure has become less transparent, not more.

The result of this is that deep systemic issues do not get addressed. As we saw in the preceding chapters, there are several such issues. First among these is irrational planning, with generation activities being planned where they are not required and targets being set by different agencies that have no relationship to each other. The flip side of this is underinvestment, both in the physical infrastructure of transmission and distribution, and in the human resources involved in staff for key activities (both in and outside discoms). Then there is the question of ensuring wider electrification, which continues to proceed at an extremely slow pace, and of making electricity available to those who need it, at prices they can afford and at a quality level that is sufficient to be useful. Finally, there is mismanagement by discoms.

Not only do these problems continue, it is now no longer clear who, if anybody, is responsible for addressing them. In the earlier system, most of them came under the State Electricity Board. Now, they are no one's responsibility. The only possible entity for addressing them is the regulatory commissions; and this too requires that these commissions will, of their own accord, be extremely rigorous and proactive.

An additional twist on this system is that the entire machinery—from procedures to commission structure to tariff fixing—is designed to incentivise private sector involvement, in order to bring in private investment. But the majority of the system at every level, generation, transmission and distribution, continues to be in the public sector. Taken at the aggregate at the national level, it is only in generation that there is significant private involvement at all. This creates a double paradox—institutions ostensibly meant to insulate private sector companies from "political interference" are now insulating the public sector from accountability, and the private sector is not providing the massive investment flows that were the reason its involvement was invited in the first place (whatever the reasons for that failure might be).

This is not to say that the earlier system was "good" and the present one "bad." In the next Chapter we return to the question of how this situation can be addressed. However, it is important to note the gulf between what the Electricity Act ostensibly set out to achieve and what has actually occurred.

2. Opportunities for Regulatory Arbitrage

The second feature of the system is that, at several points in the supply chain, there are opportunities for 'regulatory arbitrage'—taking advantage of the rules in order to make additional profits. As discussed in the previous chapter, the only clear mandate that all the bodies in this opaque and confusing structure share is to ensure that investors are able to receive a minimum guaranteed return on their investments. This is the one principle that the Electricity Act reiterates again and again, especially for the regulatory commissions. There is no other mandate beyond vague exhortations to ensure 'consumer interest.'

A similar mandate exists for those parts of the electricity system that are not technically under the Act—particularly the environmental and forest clearance systems, which are constantly being 'reformed' in the interests of improving the 'ease of doing business.' A clear message is given to financial, environmental and land authorities that promoting private investment is their goal—whatever the quality of that investment and whether it achieves its claimed goals or not.

Taken together, these mandates create a strong incentive for speculation and profiteering. A combination of a guaranteed profit without monitoring of outcomes means playing games with the rules is very profitable. In the case of generation, as discussed in detail in Chapter 3, this can mean sitting on clearances and land in order to make profits through speculation. Or it can mean manipulating the system in order to get additional profits, as in the "compensatory tariffs" for Adani Power and Tata Power discussed in the last chapter. Or it can mean straightforward corruption and deceit, as in the overinvoicing scam. In all cases the regulatory bodies have neither the capacity, nor the mandate, nor the political support to stop such activities—and in the case of the environmental regulators, they do not even see it as part of their responsibility in the first place.

The net result, as discussed in Chapter 3, is to create a regulatory system that encourages fixing, corruption, speculation and wastage rather than effective provision of services. This is once again directly contrary to the stated purpose of the Electricity Act.

If this is true, how does the system work at all? We return to this question in the last part of this chapter.

3. Environmental Destruction and Exploitation

The final destructive tendency of the system as a whole is a consequence of the above two tendencies together. This is that the system tends to encourage widespread environmental destruction and exploitation of poorer communities and the working class, both in generation and in distribution.

Two properties of the system encourage such destruction and speculation. The first is the speculation and arbitrage discussed above. Speculative activities are inherently destructive and exploitative. Speculation on coal mines or hydropower, for instance, can result in communities being displaced as their land is acquired or diverted for projects that may never come into existence (and therefore would not provide even the small benefits they may have promised). In Chapter 3 we noted how three hydropower projects in Uttarakhand that were studied in detail by the researchers did not provide any of the benefits they promised (except partially in one case, to which we return below).[1] Projects that come into operation without consideration of their impacts and costs can be even more destructive, as in the case of the Uttarakhand hydropower projects' contribution to the devastating 2013 floods.

The second property is more deep-rooted in the nature of the system itself—and doesn't require that private parties be involved. The opacity of the electricity system and the lack of any clear form of political responsibility has a direct effect on the kind of politics that forms around electricity issues. There is no single target for those affected to raise their concerns before, and instead both discontent and opposition become fragmented. This both permits and encourages political parties to effectively play games with the electricity issue. Protests and opposition by those being displaced or killed by generation projects is pitted against the interests of those who are not receiving adequate supply. Nuclear power plants are justified by saying that the country's poor need cheap and reliable electricity, coal mines are spun as vital to the interests of those who still don't have electricity connections, and easy licenses to private companies are described as vital to development. Equally, when people who are faced with power cuts and tariff hikes protest, the state and the corporate sector respond by blaming environmental regulations, anti-displacement movements, and "foreign NGOs."

This kind of political buck passing means that holding either the system or the political leadership accountable becomes far more difficult. It allows speculation and illegal profiteering to continue, while the systemic issues described in the first part of this Chapter remain unaddressed. It also means that any leader who undertakes one reform wins instant popularity—and can then afford to allow other problems to continue or become worse (the classic example of this is Narendra Modi's BJP government in Gujarat, whose decision to undertake feeder segregation in distribution became a mask for hiding the fact that Gujarat's electrification rates are still lower than comparable states and that profiteering by big private companies in the state continues). Thus the electricity system becomes a political tool for dividing, fragmenting and deflecting pressure from below.

4. Where Real Politics Affects the Electricity System

Naturally all of these factors lead to a question—if the situation is this bad, why do we have a working system at all? Why is the situation not worse? Why does it appear to indeed be improving, at least in terms of electricity supply? From our study we can only reach one conclusion—that the *actual,* real and concrete *regulation* of the electricity system is not contained in the formal and legal bodies that are responsible for it, but in a much wider and more obscure process.

Why does this happen? For two reasons. Notwithstanding both the fragmentation process described above and the ostensible "independence" of the regulatory commissions, no institution of any state is truly "independent" or "autonomous." All institutions respond to pressures from both the powerful and those affected by their decisions—it is the manner and openness of their response that varies. This, too, is a regulatory process. Fear of protest, corruption by elites, and political pressure are also regulatory in nature. We could refer to this larger system as the *political regulatory system.*

In the case of the electricity sector, we can see this clearly in how actual regulatory decisions occur. For instance, if the standard model that we discussed in Chapter 1 was correct-and almost every official and private sector analyst claims that it is—discoms across India should have vastly hiked prices. Why did they not do so? As they were afraid of public protest. This fear is not unwarranted, considering that every major tariff hike is met by protests, and such protests have forced states as diverse as Rajasthan, Bihar and Tamil Nadu to roll back tariff hikes (in February 2017, March 2017 and April 2012 respectively).

The reluctance to massively hike tariffs is then lamented by the financial press as being the result of "lack of political will", but this is merely a statement of what is happening, not an explanation for it. Indeed, in our detailed examination in Chapters 5 and 6, it emerges that the discoms may neither need to undertake such vast hikes, nor would such hikes necessarily help. Moreover, given the findings of our field survey, a massive hike would have devastating impacts on those who need electricity the most. In that sense, the political regulatory system is actually *blocking* an incorrect decision by the formal system.

This contrast is even more stark in the case of resource regulation. In Chapter 3, the utter failure of the environmental and forest clearance systems (which clear more than 99% of the projects that approach them) was discussed. Projects that are in fact stopped are halted by protest on the ground—mostly by local communities. In this sense, the only really effective environmental regulation on electricity generation in India is through public protest.

Of course the political regulatory system is not only about responding to public pressure. It is equally manifest in corruption and responses to pressure from corporate lobbies and the private sector. Here, once again, the failure of both the CERC and the appellate tribunal to halt the blatant profiteering of Adani Power and Tata Power—or to take notice of the overinvoicing for coal by over 40 generation companies—is another sign of the political regulatory system trumping the formal one, but this time in the opposite direction.

In this view, the "independence" guaranteed by the Electricity Act is actually a smokescreen. Pressure from multiple forces continues to operate, and decisions continue to be political. But these decisions are simply not taken through the formal channel. Indeed, the formal channel, as we saw above, specifically provides encouragement to private capital while blocking resistance to it. The result is not that resistance vanishes but that it fragments and operates through other channels instead. The actual governance structure that results bears little resemblance to the formal one, around which it operates as a kind of giant shadow.

It is this regulatory and political situation, rather than merely technical or policy failures, that underlies the most serious failures in India's electricity system.

Endnote

1. Chauhan and Gopalakrishnan, *The Fallacy of 'Balance' and the Irrationality of India's Resource Policies.*

8

Alternatives and Ways Forward

Most explorations of India's electricity system end with what are essentially policy recommendations. We wanted to end this book a little differently. If our analysis in the preceding Chapter is correct, the actual regulatory system extends well beyond official policy, and hence will require political action—in the sense of action to change power relations—rather than just paper changes to policies and regulations. From this perspective, the implications of our analysis will vary depending on who is reading this book. Questions of the way forward will get different answers depending on the level for which they are asked. Hence, in this chapter, we explore some possible options at multiple levels.

In all these suggestions, we have tried to keep certain principles in mind. The first of these is that the problems with the electricity system are fundamentally *structural*, not purely technical or financial. The second is that these structural problems can be tackled by trying to reduce the unaccountable, opaque and profiteering tendencies of the current system. In order to do so, we hold that we need to increase the levels of transparency—to the public; accountability—to those affected; and democracy—for all; within the system.

Some of these steps might seem small in proportion to the scale of the problem. But at each scale, it is important to act in a manner that is possible, rather than seeking policy implementation or actions that are out of proportion to one's strength. Through such strategic actions at each level, larger change might become possible.

1. For Small Organisations and Individual Electricity Consumers

Groups and individuals that consume electricity can use the spaces that exist within the existing system towards these goals.

These include, first, the use of provisions for public engagement. Public hearings are one particularly good forum. But to be most useful, these spaces need to be used to hold the generation / transmission / distribution companies and the regulatory commission accountable. Hence, it is not enough to complain either of high tariffs or to demand general improvements in electricity supply—which is what most of those who engage with these processes do. Such questions make it easy to escape accountability by providing rhetorical answers. Rather, the discom in particular can be asked to account for its own decision-making.

From the preceding chapters, some questions emerge that need particularly close examination—through, for instance, right to information requests. These points include:

- What proportion of the discom's expenditure has been spent on merchant/spot power? Why was this necessary, and why were PPAs not tied up for this power?
- How much has the discom spent on unscheduled interchange fees for short term power purchase?
- What is the staff strength of the discom and what steps are being taken to ensure that it is adequate, or to increase it?
- What proportion of metres are defective or broken, and what is being done about this?

- How much are discoms spending on interest payments on loans already taken, and what steps have been taken to reduce these?

The answers to these questions are likely to be of interest to many people. They can be given to the press and to local politician or other actors for raising these issues. Such strategies are likely to be more effective than generic complaints.

In addition to holding the discom or the regulatory commission accountable, steps can also be taken on issues of supply and quality. For instance, RTIs can establish what rules, if any, the discom has for ensuring that connections are provided within a fixed time period (a key step to minimise corruption), and for compensation to those whose appliances are damaged by power cuts or voltage fluctuations. Both are likely to exist—in particular the provision of connections within a time period—but few people will be aware of them. A follow up question can then establish how many, if any at all, officials have been proceeded against for violating these provisions. Awareness raising around these issues, again through the press and other channels, can result in a more accountable system for working class and poor people—who are otherwise ignored in most discussions around the power sector.

2. For Larger Organisations in Areas Affected by Generation Projects

Where coal mines, thermal power plants, hydroelectric projects and similar projects, the key challenge is to minimise illegal resource grabbing and to hold these projects accountable for their commitments.

For resource grabbing, two key instruments that can be used in this process are the provisions of the Forest Rights Act and the environment clearance process. The former is stronger, but it only applies where forest land is being diverted for a project. In such areas, the Forest Rights Act requires that two conditions must be met. The first is that the process of recording of rights under the FRA must be complete in the area being diverted for the project—and this must be certified by a resolution of the gram sabha (assembly of all the residents of the village) with a minimum 50% quorum. The second condition is that the informed consent of the affected gram sabhas must also be taken, again with a minimum 50% quorum.

Both these conditions are routinely violated, as we saw in Chapter 3. An easy way to check the first condition—the completion of the process of recognition of rights—is to check, using RTI, if any rights certificates have been given for rights over community forest resources under Section 3(1)(i) of the Act to any of the affected villages. Under Rule 12B(3) of the Forest Rights Rules, 2007 (as amended in 2012), this is mandatory for every village with forest dwellers in it. So if it has not been done, that is clear evidence that the process has not been completed. Similarly, the consent of the gram sabhas must be taken after informing them of the nature of the project, and after they have certified that rights recognition is complete. Have such resolutions been passed?

Similarly, the environmental clearance process provides for public hearings to be held before grant of environmental clearance. Unlike a gram sabha resolution, though, neither the consent of those attending nor any quorum is prescribed, and it is easy for generation companies and government agencies to ignore what is said. But by obtaining these records, inadequacies and problems can be revealed.

Once this information is available, it can be used to increase accountability through various channels, such as through public protest, the Environment Ministry, the press, or, as a last resort, the courts. For both of these measures, we have only touched on the legal complexities involved.

On both, however, detailed useful information and guides are available online.[1]

Of course, none of this can be done lightly. Generation companies are very powerful and their projects are lucrative for all the interests involved. This is not an easy fight and needs adequate organisational preparation and political strategy, which is one reason that we have not attempted to prescribe a more detailed strategy here; the circumstances will differ in each case.

Environmental and forest clearances apply to all large projects, but there are additional areas that can be checked in order to hold generation projects in particular to account. For instance, in the case of thermal power plants, is fuel supply available? Is it likely to involve more projects that may result in more destruction? Will hydropower projects have implications downstream, and what has been done to prepare for siltation? Are run of the river projects likely to produce near their stated capacity, or has this not been checked? Obtaining information on these points, and making it part of the public debate, can be crucial to holding such projects accountable.

3. For Larger Organisations in General

Larger organisations working in both generation areas and in other areas can explore more complex and potentially more powerful steps towards changing the electricity system—specifically towards making the system not only more accountable, but also more collective and democratic in nature.

Generation of electricity through cooperative production, using renewable energy, is one type of action that can be tried in most areas. Solar and, where feasible, microhydel projects are both amenable to this kind of production. In both cases, official promotion of renewable energy means that special financing is often available. For instance, where a microhydel project is owned by a village panchayat, the central government will bear 90% of the capital cost under the policy for small hydroelectric projects. Similarly, the cost of solar panels is currently subsidised in proportion to the tariff at which the owner will sell power to the grid.

On their own, renewable energy projects are only technically better than standard projects. But structural change can be sought by bringing these projects under wider ownership. A good way to do this is contained in the Companies Act, which—in its 2013 version—brings forward earlier provisions dealing with "producer companies" (Part IXA of the old Companies Act, 1956, brought forward by Section 465(1) of the new law). These 'companies' consist of producers themselves, who hold shares in the company. Shareholders cannot sell or buy shares, only those who fit the company's membership criteria can be shareholders, and each shareholder has only one vote, regardless of how much they have invested in the company. Section 581B(1)(f) of the Companies Act specifically says that such a company can be set up for the "generation, transmission or distribution of electricity."

Two of the present authors have been involved in setting up such a company in Chhatiara in Tehri Garhwal district, Uttarakhand, for the purpose of owning and operating a microhydel project.[2] The advantage of producer companies is clearly apparent—the law provides for a collectively owned 'company' which is internally democratic and in which all revenues are equally divided. A rough back of the envelope calculation indicated that the Chhattiara project might be able to pay Rs. 18,000 per month for each of the village's families—which is more than the current total income of many of the families in the village—as well as provide free electricity to them (which they would be entitled to as owners of the plant).

Similar structures can also be set up for collective solar energy plants and biomass incineration plants. All of this offers an alternative to the current profiteering systems in place around generation. We are not arguing that they will be able to substitute for all generation activities, but, where possible, they can replace them with genuine developmental initiatives where both electricity supply and generation can be more effective and democratic. These can then be beginnings towards changing the electricity system in a more democratic direction.

They can also become the basis of fighting for policy changes that alter the electricity system itself. For instance, after many years of pressure from social movements, in January 2015 the Uttarakhand government notified a new policy, under which all projects of under two megawatts in size in the state are reserved for ownership by gram panchayats. Talks have also been held, and tentative support received, for a demand that panchayats should be required to set up producer companies to run these projects. Though only a handful of projects have been approved under this new policy so far, it represents a step forward.

Linked to the idea of collectively owned generation projects is the often-mentioned use of "microgrids", or small local grids, as an alternative to the national grid. Microgrids offer several advantages over the national grid—they can be more efficient, they can use renewable energy for local generation, and in remote areas they can obviate the need for a connection to the main grid entirely. They can also be operated on a collective or cooperative basis.

But organisations that would attempt to experiment with microgrids need to be aware of several potential problems with these networks. First, their legal status is entirely unclear. The Electricity Act empowers panchayats, self help groups, cooperatives and other such entities to run distribution networks without a license in areas which the state government has notified as "rural." Even where such a notification has occurred—and we were not able to locate any examples of this—there is no clarity on who is responsible for safety; whether tariffs will be left to the grid operator or any regulation is possible; and, if the microgrid is powered by renewable energy, how subsidies should be claimed.[3] Furthermore, in one now infamous location where Greenpeace set up a solar-powered microgrid, the microgrid proved so expensive and unreliable that the community flocked to grid electricity when it became available.[4]

The policy questions on this front are likely to be partially addressed by a draft policy on microgrids that was made public in June 2016.[5] But this policy remains extremely vague on most of the key questions above—for instance, it simply says that, where microgrids are not connected to the grid,competition is expected to ensure that exorbitant tariffs will not be charged. In case of grievances ,the policy just states that state governments should handle such grievances through their "State Nodal Agencies"—which in most cases are renewable energy agencies that are unlikely to have the capacity to handle such questions. Regulatory commissions are expected to make regulations for safety and technical standards, but there is no clarity on who will enforce these standards, since microgrids that are not connected to the national grid are not under the Regulatory Commisions' jurisdiction. Such vague and contradictory provisions, if part of the final policy, will put some grid operators at risk of litigation. Furthermore, the draft policy barely addresses the technical and financial difficulties involved in running a microgrid. Organisations that do adopt this path need to be conscious of these problems and ensure that they adopt this approach only if they have strategies in place to deal with them.

A final area of intervention that larger organisations can contemplate, and that was briefly attempted in Chhattisgarh, is to open a dialogue with genuine unions of electricity sector workers in discoms and generation plants. These unions have an in-depth internal understanding of the sector, and also can work together with other organisations on policy changes. One difficulty in this regard is internal rivalry between multiple unions and the fact that many unions have limited their focus to wage and regularisation demands. Pushing these unions towards larger struggles, such as those outlined in this section, may be difficult. But if it becomes possible, change in the sector becomes considerably more feasible.

4. Policy Level Changes

Perhaps the most controversial conclusion that our analysis reaches is that there is indeed a need to address the problem of private sector participation in electricity—but it needs to be in the opposite direction to current policy. We have seen nearly one and a half decades of policy changes driven purely by the stated need to incentivise private sector involvement, even as we continue to have an electricity system in which distribution and transmission are almost public sector monopolies. In this sense, rather than continue to obfuscate and centralise the system in the name of privatisation, moves towards a formal renationalisation may be much more productive.

Such moves have also been considered in other countries, most notably the UK, where a 2013 poll found that 68% of the population supports renationalisation of the electricity sector, and the leadership of the main opposition Labour Party has demanded such renationalisation.[6] Latin America has also seen similar debates, and Bolivia renationalised its electricity sector in 2012. Other countries, such as Germany and Argentina, are working towards 'hybrid' systems of electricity provision.

In the Indian context, renationalisation can be progressive and can focus on distribution and transmission to begin with—which, as said, are almost entirely in state hands to begin with. In such a new governance structure, regulatory commissions would function more as ombudsmen and safeguards for public interest, which, again, is in any case the majority of their role at present (where they choose to perform it).

Renationalisation would end the process of never-ending obfuscation that has damaged the electricity sector at present and align political realities, as discussed in the previous chapter, with formal institutions. Rather than governments passing the buck to discoms or regulatory commissions, they would need to take responsibility for their decisions. They would also be both empowered to, and responsible for, investment and maintenance of infrastructure as well as the consequences of destructive generation projects. This could involve transitions towards a stronger grid capable of handling the challenges from renewable and microgrid installations.

This should not be taken to mean we are suggesting a return to the pre-1998 State Electricity Board system. Rather, keeping in mind the principles outlined at the beginning of this chapter, a much more democratic and collective approach can be adopted that is based on the principles of publication of all accounts, democratic decision-making over generation, and collective control over distribution. As long as private generation remains a major player, this should also include steps to curb speculation through tighter control over credit and finance to generation projects—especially those that have not received environmental clearances or the consent of local communities.

Of course, at present, such a policy project is essentially a pipe dream, which is also why we are perforce required to keep it vague. Hence we also return to the point mentioned at the beginning of this chapter—the priority for now is not generic policy recommendations but the *political* steps necessary to make such larger shifts possible at all. Only then can we begin the long journey towards a better, more just system of electricity provision in India.

Endnotes

1. For FRA-related provisions, see www.forestrightsact.com. For environment clearances, see www.ercindia.org and other similar websites.
2. At the time of writing, this company has received preliminary sanction, and a detailed project report is now being prepared by a consultant hired by the central government.
3. Sudha Mahalingam, "How Private Mini-Grids Can End the Darkness of Rural India," *The Wire* (27 June 2016).
4. Gayatri Vaidyanathan, "Coal Trumps Solar in India," *Scientific American* (19 October 2015).
5. "Draft National Policy for Renewable Energy Based Micro and Mini Grids", 1 June, 2016, Ministry of Power.
6. Tom Bawden, "Should the Big Six Be Renationalised?" *The Independent* (3 December 2013); Matt Dathan, "Labour Leadership: Jeremy Corbyn Pledges to Renationalise the Big Six Energy Firms," *The Independent* (7 August 2015).

References

Agarwal, Rakesh. "Hydropower Projects in Uttarakhand." *Economic and Political Weekly* 48, No. 29 (20 July 2013).

Anandane, Uma Maheshwari. "India's Largest Blackout in History." *Powercuts.In* (4 October 2012). http://blog.powercuts.in/?p=28.

Annamalai, Thillai. "Merchant Power Plants in India: Risk Analysis Using Simulation." *International Journal of Energy Sector Management* (December 2009).

Asthana, Shishir. "UDAY Is a Revival Plan for Discoms Rather Than a Bailout Package." *Business Standard* (6 November 2015).

Bawden, Tom. "Should the Big Six Be Renationalised?" *The Independent* (3 December 2013).

Bhaskar, Utpal. "CERC Plans to Further Narrow Frequency Band for National Grid." *Mint* (30 July 2013).

CAG. *Performance of Special Economic Zones*. Comptroller and Auditor General, 2014. http://www.saiindia.gov.in/english/home/Our_Products/Audit_Report/Government_Wise/union_audit/recent_reports/union_performance/2014/INDT/Report_21/Report_21.html.

Campaign for Survival and Dignity. "Bringing Back the British Raj in Forests," 15 September 2014. https://forestrightsact.com/2014/09/15/bringing-back-the-british-raj-in-forests/.

Chauhan, Trepan Singh, and Shankar Gopalakrishnan. *The Fallacy of 'Balance' and the Irrationality of India's Resource Policies*. Social Research Collective, July 2015. http://srcindia.wordpress.com.

Chhatre, Ashwini. *Land Disputes and Stalled Investments in India*. Rights Resources Initiative, 16 November 2016.

Chitnis, Ashwini, and Shantanu Dixit. "It's Time to End the 'Bid Low, Raise Prices Later' Strategy of Power Sector Players." *The Wire* (27 April 2016).

Choudhury, Rita Roy, Priyanka Dhingra, Rathin Roy, Vivan Sharan, and Nick Robins. *Delivering a Sustainable Financial System in India*. Inquiry Report. UNEP FICCI, April 2016.

Commonwealth Foundation. *Making It Flow: Learning from Commonwealth Experiences in Water and Electricity Provision*. Commonwealth Foundation, 2004.

Comptroller and Auditor General. *Performance Audit of Hydropower Development Through Private Sector Participation*. Government of Uttarakhand, 31 March 2009.

CSE. "Coal Mining." Centre for Science and Environment, 22 September 2011. http://www.cseindia.org/userfiles/Coal%20mining.pdf.

____. "Thermal Power Plants." Centre for Science and Environment, 22 September 2011. http://www.cseindia.org/userfiles/Thermal%20 power%20plant.pdf.

Dathan, Matt. "Labour Leadership: Jeremy Corbyn Pledges to Renationalise the Big Six Energy Firms." *The Independent* (7 August 2015).

Datta, Sanjay. "Bill to Amend Electricity Act Put on Back Burner." *Times of India* (12 October 2015).

Dixit, Shantanu, and Ann Josey. "No Sunrise Just Yet." *Indian Express* (21 November 2015).

ET. "How UDAY is Going to Help Transform India's Power Distribution System." *Economic Times* (25 October 2016).

____. "India's Looming Power Crisis." *Economic Times* (19 February 2016).

FICCI. *Power Transmission: The Real Bottleneck*. Federation of Indian Chambers of Commerce and Industry, 2013.

Fine, Ben, and Ellen Leopold. *The World of Consumption*. Routledge, 1993.

Greenpeace. *Mining Impacts*, 11 April 2010. http://www.greenpeace.org/international/en/campaigns/climate-change/coal/Mining-impacts/.

Harish, Santosh M., and Shuba V. Raghavan. "Redesigning the National Solar Mission for Rural India." *Economic and Political Weekly* (4 June 2011).

Himachal Live Service. "Higher Silt Level Shuts Down SJVNL Power Project." *Himachal Times* (20 July 2010).

Himanshu Thakkar. *There Is Little Hope Here: Critique on India's Climate Plan*. South Asian Network on Dams, Rivers; People, 2009.

IANS. "UDAY Scheme Will Impact People Negatively—Jayalalitha." *Times of India* (11 April 2016).

Jai, Shreya. "The Trouble with Electricity Regulator." *Business Standard* (8 March 2015).

Jayaraman, Nityanand. "'Ex-Post Facto Prior Environmental Clearances': How a Nonsensical Phrase Was Used to Flout the Law." *Scroll.in* (11 July 2015).

Jayaraman, Nityanand, and Mukul Kumar. "There Is No Power Shortage in the Country—But the Entire Sector is in a Mess." *Scroll.in* (18 August 2016). https://scroll.in/article/814192/there-is-no-power-shortage-in-the-country-but-the-entire-sector-is-in-a-mess.

Kasturi, Kannan. "Is the Government's Overly Aggressive Solar Thrust in Public Interest?" Journal. *Economic and Political Weekly*, Vol. 52, Issue No. 6 (2017).

____. "Pricing Electricity in Delhi." *Economic and Political Weekly*, Vol. 48, Issue No. 1 (5 January 2013).

Khanna, Ashish. *Lighting Rural India: Experience of Rural Load Segregation Schemes in States*. World Bank, 2013.

Kohli, Kanchi, Manju Menon, Sanchari Das, and Divya Badami. *Calling the Bluff: Revealing the State of Monitoring and Compliance of Environmental Clearance Conditions*. Kalpavriksh, 2009.

KPMG. *Power Sector in India: White Paper on Challenges in Implementation and Opportunities*. KPMG, 2010.

Krithika, P.R., and S. Mahajan. *Background Paper on Governance of Renewable Energy in India: Issues and Challenges*. TERI, March 2014.

Kulkarni, J.D. "Business Landscape." *Power Watch India* (n.d.). http://powerwatchindia.com/business-landscape/.

Kumar, Subhash. "Interview on the UERC and the Power Situation in Uttarakhand." Chairperson, Uttarakhand Electricity Regulatory Commission, Interview, April 2016.

Lazarus, Michael, and Chelsea Chandler. "Coal Power in the CDM: Issues and Options." Stockholm Environment Institute, November 2011.

Madhu, Maulik. "'Cheaper Electricity Is Not That Easy'." *The Hindu* (10 July 2016).

Mahalingam, Sudha. "How Private Mini-Grids Can End the Darkness of Rural India." *The Wire* (27 June 2016).

Manshi Asher. "Buying Silence, Manufacturing Consent." *InfochangeIndia.org* (20 December 2011). http://infochangeindia.org/water-resources/features/buying-silence-manufacturing-consent.html.

McKinsey. *Powering India: The Road to 2017*. McKinsey Co., 2005.

Ministry of Power. *Report of the Enquiry Committee on Grid Disturbance in the Northern Region on 30 July 2012*. Ministry of Power, 2012. http://powermin.nic.in/sites/default/files/uploads/GRID_ENQ_REP_16_8_12.pdf.

Mishra, Neelkanth. "The UDAY Plug-in." *Indian Express* (17 March 2016).

Muruganandham, T. "Centre Blinks, Tamil Nadu to Join UDAY Scheme by Year End." *New Indian Express* (22 October 2016).

Overdorf, Jason. "How Many Dams Can One State Hold?" *Global Post* (2012). http://www.globalpost.com/dispatch/news/regions/asia-pacific/india/120315/dam-nation-arunachal-pradesh-hydropower-electricity-part-1.

Paliwal, Ankur. "Separate Power Feeders Can Greatly Improve Rural Electrification." *Down to Earth* (October 7 2013).

Pandey, Vivek. "Electricity Grid Management in India—An Overview." *Electrical India* 47, No. 11 (November 2007).

Pargal, Sheoli, and Sudeshna Ghosh Banerjee. *More Power to India: The Challenge of Electricity Distribution*. World Bank, 2014.

Pillay, Amritha. "Costly Imported Coal Squeeze Power Producers' Margins." *Business Standard* (n.d.).

Prayas. *Know the Electricity Act 2003*. Prayas Energy Research Group, n.d. http://www.prayaspune.org.

Raja, John Samuel, and M. Rajshekhar. "Coal Block Allocations: Private Profiteering from a Public Asset." *Economic Times* (7 August 2012).

Rajan, Raghuram. "Raghuram Rajan: Large Wilful Promoter Defaults Robs Taxpayers." *Business Standard* (27 November 2014).

Rajshekhar, M. "Over 50 Coal Blocks Allotted to Private Companies Have Been Sold: Hansraj Ahir." *Economic Times* (13 July 2012).

Rajshekhar, M. "Chhattisgarh Power Boom That Never Was: Only 15 Out of 60 Thermal Plants May Get Operational." *Economic Times* (25 October 2012).

____. "Hydelgate: Why Arunachal Pradesh's Hydel Boom Is Going Bust." *Economic Times* (30 April 2013).

RBI. *Financial Stability Report*. Reserve Bank of India; Reserve Bank of India, 2015.

Rosencranz, Armin, and Rajnish Wadehra. "The Confusion Over Coal, Power Tells Us India Hasn't Outgrown the Need for Planning." *The Wire* (18 February 2017).

Sati, Neeraj. "Interview on Electricity Situation in Uttarakhand." Secretary, Uttarakhand Electricity Regulatory Commission; Interview, April 2016.

Schlissel, David. *Bad Choice: The Risks, Costs and Viability of Proposed US Nuclear Reactors in India*. IEEFA, 30 March 2016.

Sen, Jahnavi. "The Social Realities of India's Electrification, in One Map." *The Wire* (24 January 2016).

Sen, Sandip. "How and Why the Indian Power Grid Collapsed." *Economic Times* (29 August 2012).

Sen, Shreeja, and Shailaja Sharma. "CERC Allows Tata Power, Adani Power to Pass Through High Cost." *Mint* (8 December 2016).

Sethi, Nitin. "As Forest Minister, Jairam Wasn't Anti-Industry." *Times of India*, 24 July 2011.

____. "Changes in Tribal Rights and Green Rules 'Save' 130 Mines." *Business Standard* (18 January 2017).

____. "PMO Meeting Changed NDA's Stance to Favour More Dams in Uttarakhand." *Business Standard* (12 March 2015).

Sethi, Nitin, and Ishan Bakshi. "Government Claims of Windfall Gains from Coal Auction Lack Clarity." *Business Standard* (21 April 2015).

Shah, Shreya. "One Third of UP Voters Polled Cite Power Cuts as Leading Election Issue." *India Spend* (6 February 2017).

Shankaran, Sanjiv. "Jayalalitha Torpedoes Piyush Goyal's UDAY." *Business Standard* (6 May 2016).

Sharma, Ashok. "Interview on Situation in UPCL." State Secretary, All India Trade Unions Congress; retired UPCL staff member; Interview, 26 May 2016.

Sharma, Nidhi. "Not a Single Acquisition Under Land Ordinance for Developmental Projects in Six Months." *Economic Times* (30 July 2015).

Sharma, Supriya. "CAG Report Provides Hard Evidence Why the Land Acquisition Law Should Not Be Diluted." *Scroll.in* (17 July 2014).

Shrivastava, Shruti. "Land Acquisition Legislation: Amid Central Logjam, States Move Forward." *Indian Express* (10 November 2015).

Singh, Sarita. "UDAY a Success: India's Power Distribution System Shows Clear Signs of Revival." *Economic Times* (3 October 2016).

Singh, Yudhvir. "Presentation to National Consultation on Takeover of Common Lands." Society for Promotion of Wasteland Development, July 2011.

Srivas, Anuj. "It's Time to Shift the Rural Electrification Goalpost." *The Wire* (12 April 2016).

Standing Committee on Energy. *Report of the Standing Committee on Energy on the Electricity (Amendment) Bill, 2014*. Lok Sabha, 2015. http://164.100.47.193/lsscommittee/Energy/16_Energy_4.pdf.

Suchitra, M. "Green Energy Takes Toll on Green Cover." *Down to Earth* (3 October 2011).

Thakurta, Paranjoy Guha. "How Over-Invoicing of Imported Coal Has Increased Power Tariffs." Journal. *Economic and Political Weekly* Vol. 51, Issue No. 15 (2016).

____. "Power Tariff Scam Gets Bigger at Rs. 50,000 Crore." Journal. *Economic and Political Weekly* Vol. 51, Issue No. 20 (2016).

UERC. *Order on Approval of Business Plan and Multi Year Tariff Petition for Uttarakhand Power Corporation Ltd. for Second Control Period (Fy 2016-2017 to Fy 2018-2019)*. Uttarakhand Electricity Regulatory Commission, 5 April 2016.

Vaidyanathan, Gayatri. "Coal Trumps Solar in India." *Scientific American* (19 October 2015).

Vishnoi, Anubhuti. "Is Modi Government's Target to Increase Solar Power Capacity Five Fold in Seven Years Achievable?" *Economic Times* (22 August 2015).